Hidden Mysteries

Hidden Mysteries

Hindi Collection of Talks

Gahre Pani Paith

OSHO

PAN

This edition published 2019 by Pan
an imprint of Pan Macmillan Publishing India Private Limited,
707, Kailash Building
26 K. G. Marg, New Delhi – 110 001
www.panmacmillan.co.in

Pan Macmillan, The Smithson, 6 Briset Street, London EC1M 5NR
Associated companies throughout the world
www.panmacmillan.com

ISBN 978-93-86215-93-2

Originally published in Hindi under the title: *Gahre Pani Paith*

The material in this book is from a series of talks by Osho given to a live audience. The complete OSHO text archive can be found via the online OSHO Library at www.osho.com

1 0

Typeset by Manmohan Kumar
Printed and bound in India by Repro India Ltd

FSC
www.fsc.org
MIX
Paper from responsible sources
FSC® C047271

Contents

Suppose we have a key in our hands. We cannot directly understand the purpose of it from the key itself . . . There are many such keys in life which even today can open the doors to treasures, but unfortunately we neither know anything about these treasures nor about the locks which may be opened.

– OSHO

Preface

Religion is only for those who are ready to enter into the impossible. Religion is for the gamblers, not for the shopkeepers. Religion is neither a business deal nor a compromise. Religion is a wager. A gambler puts his wealth at stake; the religious person puts himself at stake because that is the ultimate wealth.

One who is not ready to stake his very life will never be able to know the hidden mysteries of life. Those secrets are not available cheaply. Knowledge is available very cheaply; knowledge is available from books, from scriptures, in education, with the teachers. Knowledge is available almost for free; you do not have to pay anything for it. In religion you have to pay heavily. It is not right even to say "heavily" because only when someone stakes everything do the doors to that life open. The doors to that life open only for those who put this life at stake. To put this life at stake is the only key to the door of that life.

Osho

Finger Pointing to the Moon

1
Hidden Mysteries of Eastern Temples

Beloved Osho,
There was a time when temples, places of pilgrimage, the wearing of forehead marks, idol worship, the use of rosaries, incantations and spells, scriptures, rituals and astrology, a belief in good and bad omens – all had a meaning. Now, however, they have become meaningless. Please, explain them to us. We would also like to know if these were all only the outer tools of spiritual discipline, merely the outer arrangements to trigger a remembrance, whose meaning has been totally lost with the passage of time, or had they some intrinsic value? Will there be a time when they will be used again?

SUPPOSE WE HAVE A KEY IN OUR HANDS. We cannot directly understand the purpose of it from the key itself, nor is it possible to imagine from the key itself that a great treasure is likely to be revealed with its help. There is no hidden indication in the key regarding the treasure; the key itself is closed. Even if we break it or cut it into pieces, we may find the metal of which it is made, but we cannot learn anything about the hidden treasure which the key is capable of revealing. And whenever such a key – without any clues as to the treasure – is preserved for a long time, it only becomes a burden on our life.

There are many such keys in life which even today can open the doors to treasures, but unfortunately we neither know anything about these treasures nor about the locks which may be opened. And if we do not know about either the treasures or the locks, then what is left in our hands cannot even be called a key. It can only be a key if it opens a lock. This same key may have revealed treasures sometime in the past, but because today nothing can be unlocked, the key has become a burden. And yet, somehow we still do not feel like throwing it away.

The key has left a sort of lingering fragrance in the unconscious mind of man. Maybe thousands of years ago this key did open locks, and treasures were found: the memory of that in the unconscious mind makes us carry the burden of the key to this day. However much we may be persuaded about the uselessness of the key, we cannot gather the courage to throw it away. In some unknown corner of the heart the hope still lingers that someday, some lock might be opened by it.

Take for example, temples: there is no race on earth which has not built something like a temple – it does not matter whether it is called a *masjid* or a church or a gurdwara. Today it is possible for us to learn something from other races, but there was a time when we did not even know about the existence of other races, so there was no way to learn from them. The temple is not the fanciful result of the imagination of some eccentric people; its roots lie somewhere deep in the inner consciousness of man.

He may have lived faraway in the forest, or on a mountain, or in a cave, or on the bank of a river – he may have lived anywhere for that matter – but wherever he has lived man has built something resembling a temple, something has come out of his consciousness. There is no blind imitation in it: they were not constructed by looking at other temples, so all temples have been of different shapes and types – but they have always existed.

There is a lot of difference between a temple and a *masjid*; their arrangement and design are quite different from each other. But there is no difference between men in their aspiration or inner urge. A man may be anywhere: however unfamiliar and unacquainted he is with others, still he carries the same latent seed somewhere in his consciousness.

Another thing worth noting is that though thousands of years have passed, and now we have no clue about the locks or the hidden treasures, still we continue to carry these strange keys as if under the spell of some lingering memory. Despite all the attacks on it – reason tries to shatter it from all sides, and the so-called modern intellectual does not accept it – the human heart still treasures this memory and continues to be fascinated by it. So we ought to remember that although he is not aware of it today, somewhere in man's unconscious is a resounding echo which tells him locks which used to open once existed.

Why is this stored in the unconscious? It is because none of us are new to this world. All of us are born again and again, and there was never a time when we did not exist. What we knew consciously in days past has now, today, become unconscious – buried within us under thousands of layers as the unconscious. If, in days past, we once knew the significance and deeper secrets of some temple, and had experienced the opening of some inner door, then somewhere in the deep recesses of the unconscious that memory still lies dormant. The intellect may totally deny its existence, but intellect cannot reach the depth where the memory is retained.

So despite all the obstacles, despite its apparent meaninglessness, it is something which persists, which cannot be removed. It may take new forms, but it continues. Still, this is only possible because we have known something an infinite number of times on our infinitely long journey of births and deaths – even though we may not remember it today.

Apart from having an outward use – as a means to an end – each of these things also has a deeper significance and purpose.

The universal urge to build temples is only inherent in man. Animals make their dwellings and birds build nests, but they do not build temples. When distinguishing man from animals, one prominent feature is that man is a temple-making animal – no other animal makes temples. To provide some shelter for oneself is absolutely natural – it is done by every creature; birds and animals do it, even small insects do it – but to build a house for the divine is a distinctive feature of man.

Without man having some deep awareness of the divine, a temple could not be built. Even if that awareness is later lost, the temple still remains; and it is quite certain it could not have been built without a deep experience of the divine.

You make a guesthouse because guests go on visiting you – if there were no guests, you would not waste money on a guesthouse – and even though there may be no guests visiting now, the guesthouse remains. So the whole idea of building temples or shrines for the divine must have been conceived of in such moments when the divine was not just a matter of imagination for people, but a living experience. The very phenomenon of the incarnation of the divine on earth made it necessary to have special places, in every nook and corner of the planet, that could serve as special dwellings for him. To properly receive someone, adequate arrangements have to be made.

It can be understood this way: radio waves are passing all around us, but they cannot be picked up without a radio receiver. If tomorrow there was a Third World War and all technology was destroyed, yet luckily somehow a radio receiver was left intact, you would not want to throw it away. Even though you would know you could not broadcast, or tune in to any program, or even find a technician to repair it, you would not want to throw the radio away.

After several generations of your family, if anyone was to ask the use of the radio, none of the family members alive would be able to reply. They might only say their fathers and their forefathers were insistent on its being preserved, so they continue to keep it. Their forefathers never told them what it was for, they don't know its use, and so it is of no help to them. Even if the radio were to be dismantled, nothing could be known about it. By opening the radio, one could not know that some time in the past, music and talking could be heard through it. This radio had once acted as a receiving station for something happening elsewhere; it could pick up the waves and act as a medium, presenting them as sounds to listeners.

In exactly the same manner, temples once functioned as receptive instruments. Though godliness is everywhere and human beings are also present everywhere, only during specific circumstances within us do we become attuned to that godliness. So temples served as centers of receptivity, to enable us to feel the divine in existence, to feel godliness, and to become spiritually elevated. The whole arrangement in temples was motivated with this end in view.

Different types of people thought up differing arrangements, but that is not of much consequence. It makes no difference that various manufacturers produce radios incorporating their own specialities, with different shapes and forms – the ultimate purpose is the same.

The temples in India were mostly constructed in one of three or four patterns; other temples became just copies of these. The domes of the temples were based on a model of the sky. There was an underlying purpose to this. If I sit under the open sky and repeat 'Om', my voice will be lost because the strength of an individual voice will be enveloped by the vastness of the sky. I will not be able to hear the reverberation, and the echo of my chanting – all my prayers – will get lost in the vastness of the sky.

Domes were constructed so the resonance of our prayers can rebound on us. The dome is just a small, semicircular prototype of the sky. It has the same shape as the sky touching the earth on all four sides. Whatever prayers or chanting are done under its canopy do not get lost the way they would under the vast sky, because the dome throws them back toward the worshipper. The rounder the dome, the easier it is for the sound to travel back, and its echo increases in the same proportion. As time passed, it was discovered that stone too could multiply the resonance to a tremendous degree.

There is a Buddhist prayer hall in the Ajanta caves where the stones echo sound with the same intensity as the Indian musical instrument called the tabla. If we strike the stones with the same force as is used in playing the tabla, they will give out the same volume of sound. If ordinary stone were used in the construction of domes, it cannot echo certain very subtle sounds, so this specific type of stone was used.

But what is the purpose behind all this? The purpose is that when anyone chants 'Om', and it is done very intensely, the dome of the temple makes the sound reverberate, forming a circle of the echoing sound. The temple dome, by the nature of its design, helps in the formation of a circle by echoing the sound. Such a sound circle is a blissful experience. If 'Om' is chanted under the wide open sky, no sound circle will be formed and you will never experience this bliss.

When the formation of the circle happens, you are no longer just a humble worshipper before the divine, you become a recipient as well – in other words, the one whose prayers are being answered. And with that resonance the divine experience begins to enter you. Although the sound produced in the chanting is human, when it is echoed it resounds with a new force and is full of new energies.

These dome-shaped temples were used to create sound circles through the chanting of mantras. If one chants there, sitting all alone in perfect peace and silence, then as soon as the sound circle is formed thoughts will stop. On the one hand, the circle is formed, and on the other, thoughts come to a stop. As I have often said, a circle of energy is formed even in the act of sexual intercourse between a man and a woman; and when the formation of such a circle takes place, that is the moment pointing toward superconsciousness.

Look at the statues of Buddha and Mahavira sitting in the posture of *padmasana* or *siddhasana*. They indicate other methods for the formation of such circles. When we sit putting both our feet together and our hands on our legs, the whole body begins to act as a circle. Then the body electricity cannot escape and a circuit is created. As soon as the circuit is created, one becomes thoughtless. If we use the language of an electrical engineer, it could be said that the crowd of noisy thoughts within the mind exists because we have not created an inner electrical circuit. As soon as the circuit is created, the inner energy becomes balanced and silent. So, creating a circle of energy with the help of the temple dome was a great process – and this was its purpose and deep significance.

At the entrance of temples, we find big bells or gongs and they serve the same purpose. When you chant 'Om', although you may be doing so very quietly and your attention may be elsewhere, the sound of the bell will instantly bring your attention back to the circle of sound created by its vibration. It is just like when a stone is thrown into a pond, creating ripple upon ripple.

In Tibetan temples, instead of a bell or gong they keep a bowl-shaped vessel made from various metals, and a wooden stick to revolve inside it. The stick is rotated within the vessel seven times, and then it is struck once on the bowl with a loud bang. The vibrations created in the bowl produce a sound like *Om mani padme hum* – the whole mantra. The bowl echoes the sound, *Om mani padme hum*, not once, but seven times. Turn the stick inside the bowl rapidly seven times, strike the bowl, take the stick out, and you will hear the echo of the mantra *Om mani padme hum* seven times. Though the sound will gradually become softer and softer, it will be heard seven times.

Similarly, when you intone the mantra *Om mani padme hum* in a domed temple, the temple will echo it. Every cell of your body will receive the vibration and return it with a deeper resonance. After a few moments neither you nor the temple will be there – only circles of energy will be left.

It should be remembered that sound is a subtle form of electricity, now even science agrees with this. In fact, everything is a form of electricity. But the Indian sages go one step further and say electricity is a form of sound, that sound is the base, not electricity. That is why they call the supreme being *shabda brahman* – God is sound.

There is now a great similarity of approach between Eastern thinkers and modern scientists, the only difference being just which of the two is primary. The scientist says electricity is primary, whereas the sage says it is the density of sound which produces electricity. There is every possibility that in the near future science will have to look deeper into the nature of *shabda brahman*, sound, the ultimate reality.

The sage's understanding stems from the experience of the sounds produced under the dome of a temple. When a meditator creates the intense sound of 'Om' in a temple, within a short time he will feel that neither he nor the temple is there, only electricity remains. This conclusion has not been reached in any laboratory; the people who made such declarations had no laboratories, their temple served as their only laboratory. There they experienced that even though they would start with sound, what remained in the end was electricity.

Dome-shaped temples were created in order to experience this transformation of sound. When Westerners saw Indian temples for the first time, they thought they were very unhygienic. By the very nature of their conception these temples could not have many doors and windows. There could only be one door, and that too very small. The idea behind this was to ensure the circle of sound being created in the temple did not become depleted. It is no wonder then these Westerners went away with the impression that the temples were dingy, dark and dirty, and fresh air could not enter. By comparison, their own churches were airy and clean, with many big doors and windows through which light and fresh air could easily enter, keeping them hygienic.

I have told you earlier, when the secret of using a key is forgotten, all sorts of difficulties occur. Today, not one person in India would be able to say why temples were not provided with many windows and doors. So when asked, we also feel inclined to agree our temples are unhygienic. No one now would be able to contend that the healthiest people had lived in these temples and no disease had ever been allowed to enter. Those who had prayed and worshipped there were some of the healthiest people ever, in the true sense of the term.

Why is that? Gradually it was realized that the sound produced by the chanting of 'Om' has a unique purifying effect. There are certain sounds which have a purifying effect, and there are others which contaminate. Some particular sounds act as deterrents to diseases, and there are others which invite disease. The whole science of sound has however been lost.

Those who have said 'sound is absolute being' have said the ultimate that can be said about sound. There is no experience greater than that of absolute being, and they had not known anything deeper than sound through which to express themselves.

All melodies and modes and their modifications are born in the East. They are extensions of experiencing the absolute being in the form of sound. Musical compositions, as well as all dance forms, originated in temples, and later on developed as specific arts elsewhere. It was only in the temple that a devotee experienced the effects of sound in its innumerable variations – so many that it is difficult to keep count.

Just forty years ago, a hermit called Vishuddhananda lived in Varanasi. He gave hundreds of demonstrations to prove it is possible to kill somebody using particular sounds. This man used to sit under the dome of a temple, a temple which could be said to be utterly unhygienic according to modern standards. And for the first time, in the presence of three doctors from England, an experiment was carried out. The doctors brought a sparrow into the temple with them. Vishuddhananda made certain sounds – the sparrow fluttered about for a while, and then fell down dead. The doctors examined it and pronounced it dead. Then Vishuddhananda made some other sounds – the sparrow came back to life, and began fluttering about again. It was then realized for the first time that the impact of certain sounds can produce specific effects.

Now we readily accept that certain effects are produced by certain sounds because it has been demonstrated scientifically. We now agree that if a particular light-ray falls on your body, it will have a particular effect; if a specific medicine is administered to a patient, it will produce a specific effect; if particular colors are used, they bring about particular effects. Why then shouldn't particular sounds cause certain effects?

Now there are several laboratories in the West which are actively engaged in the investigation of the relationship between sound and life; and two or three laboratories have arrived at conclusions of deep significance. In two such laboratories, scientists have proved that particular sounds can produce more milk in lactating mothers. Through certain sounds, plants can be made to blossom within two months instead of the usual six months; and cows yield more milk if soft music is played at the time of milking. Dairies in Russia today employ this latest method at the time of milking. And the day is not far off when fruit and vegetables will be grown with the help of special sounds. Laboratory demonstrations have already been made, now it is only a matter of time until it is done on a broader scale. If fruit, vegetables, and milk are influenced by sound, shouldn't we be influenced by sound?

Disease and health are determined by particular sound waves: so in the past, people made hygienic arrangements in their temples which did not depend only on air and atmosphere. They did not believe that only an abundant air supply leads to good health. Otherwise, it is inconceivable that over a period of five thousand years they would not have hit upon the idea of properly ventilating their places of worship.

The Indian hermit usually sits in caves where no light or air enters, or else he sits in temples with doors so small that one has to bend low to enter. There are some temples where you have to lie down and crawl in to enter. In spite of this, there were no ill effects on their health. In India this has been our experience over thousands of years. But when for the first time we began to doubt this, we also made our temple doors bigger and installed windows. We modernized the temples, but in doing so converted them into ordinary buildings. Their very purpose as keys to something more was lost.

The acoustics and the architecture of a temple have a deep connection. In fact, the whole thing is a science of sound. There is a specific stipulation as to the angle at which a sound is to be made. There are stipulations for making a sound while standing and while sitting. It is even stipulated which sounds can be made only while lying down – because the impact of the sound will have a certain effect when made standing and will change again when made while sitting down. It is also clarified which sounds should be made together, and which are to be made separately for different results. So it is interesting to note the confusion that was created when vedic literature was translated into Western languages.

Western languages emphasize the linguistic rather than the phonetic, whereas the vedic view gives more importance not so much to the meaning of the written or spoken word, as to the special sound it should produce, and the composition of that sound. Hence the Sanskrit language is phonetic, not linguistic – the emphasis is more on the sound than on the word. And so for thousands of years it was felt that these valuable scriptures should not be written down because it was natural that when they were written down, the emphasis on sound would be lost. The insistence was that the knowledge be passed on by word of mouth – rather than in writing – because in writing words down they would become mere words, and the subtle nuances associated with the sound would be lost and so become meaningless.

If we write down the name Rama, those who are reading it will say the word in many different ways. Someone will put more emphasis on *r* and someone else more emphasis on *a*, and still somebody else will put more emphasis on *m*. It will depend on the individual reader. So as soon as a word is written down, the effect of the sound is destroyed. Now to understand the effect of the sound of those words, a whole decoding exercise to pronounce the words correctly will have to be done. So, for thousands of years, there was a strong insistence on not writing the scriptures because the ancient seers did not want the phonetic arrangement to be lost. The scriptures had to be passed on to others directly by word of mouth, so scriptures were known as *shrutis*, meaning that which is learned by listening. What was passed down in the form of written books was never accepted as scripture.

It was all scientifically based on the arrangement of sound. At some places the sound had to be soft and at others it had to be loud. It was very difficult to write these words in script form. The day the scriptures were reduced to writing, the essential, inherent, original, and inner arrangement of the sound was lost. It was no longer necessary to understand only through listening. You can read a scripture – it is available in the market. Now there is no relationship or relevance to sound.

It is important to note that the emphasis of the scriptures was never on the meaning. The emphasis on meaning became relevant later, when we reduced those scriptures to writing. If something written down has no meaning it will look insane, so meaning has necessarily to be given to the written word. There are still some parts of vedic lore where no meaning could be deciphered – and these are the real parts because they are totally phonetic. They do not convey any meaning.

For example, no question about the meaning of the Tibetan mantra *Om mani padme hum* arises because its significance is totally phonetic. Similarly, there is no question of any meaning in the mantra 'Om', but it has a sound-based impact which creates a special effect. When a meditator repeats *Om mani padme hum* again and again, the sound affects the various chakras and they are activated. It is not a question of meaning; the significance concerns the sounds themselves. So, the fact that the old scriptures did not lay any stress on the meaning, but only on their utility – on what they could be used for and their benefits – deserves our special attention.

Buddha was once asked, 'What is truth?' He replied, 'Truth is that which can be used.' The definition of truth is: 'That which can be used.' Science will define truth in the same way. Its definition will be pragmatic: 'Truth is that which can be made use of and which can be shown.'

If it is said that water is created when hydrogen and oxygen are mixed, we don't care whether the statement is true or not – if we can see that water is made by mixing hydrogen and oxygen, it is true, otherwise not. The statement in itself has no validity – its validity is in its utility. If it is possible to create water in this way, it has to be proved by actual demonstration. Now science has adopted this definition of truth which religion accepted five thousand years ago. In religion, utility was the test to verify a truth.

The mantra 'Om' has no meaning, but it has a utility; a temple has no meaning, but it has a utility. To make use of it is an art, and there is an inherent flow in all art which cannot be taught, but must be absorbed.

I have heard . . .

There was an emperor in China fifteen hundred years ago, who was very fond of meat – so much so that he would have a cow or bull slaughtered right before his eyes. The same butcher slaughtered cattle in front of him every morning for fifteen years. One day the emperor asked, 'I haven't seen you sharpening your axe once in fifteen years. Doesn't its edge become blunt?'

The butcher replied, 'No, Your Majesty, it doesn't. The edge only becomes blunt when the butcher is not an expert – if he does not know where to strike. The butcher must know where there are bones and joints, and then the axe can cut the animal in two with one blow. This art of cutting is passed on from one generation to the next. So not only does the edge not become blunt, but it becomes sharper daily, with every fresh stroke.'

The emperor asked the butcher to teach him the art. The butcher replied, 'It would be very difficult. I have not learned this art, but imbibed it by watching my father since early childhood. It wasn't taught to me – I absorbed the art through watching my father every day. Sometimes I would fetch the axe for him, and sometimes I would stack up the limbs of the animals – that was how I learned the art. If you are ready to do the same – standing beside me, sometimes handing over the axe to me, and then putting it back, sometimes simply sitting and watching – then perhaps you will learn the art. But I cannot teach it to you.'

Science can be taught but art has to be imbibed.

All these mantras have no meaning but they have pragmatic value, and we used to make our children absorb them at a very early age. They would learn the use of the temple without ever even being aware of what they had learned. They would learn the art of entering a temple, how to sit there and how to make use of the sacred precincts. Whenever there was an emergency or any difficulties, people would run to the temple and then return home having regained a sense of balance and tranquility. Each morning they would go to the temple because it was not possible to find what they got there anywhere else. But all of this was not taught to them – they incorporated it at a very early stage in childhood. It was not taught to them but imbibed by them. Wherever there is art, it cannot be taught.

The effects of sound in the temple, and the temple itself, were an arrangement for experimentation. As long as the effect of the sound of a word was not understood, the whole experiment was meaningless.

For example, it was a convention that a mantra should only be given to a disciple by a master. The emphasis was on the mantra being recited by the master in the disciple's ear. You might have known the mantra for a long time, but still the master would whisper it in your ear.

You might wonder, 'What is new in this? Couldn't I have done it without the master? Everybody knows how to repeat a mantra, and still this master has whispered it to me as if it were a great secret!'

But what is to be understood is that when the master says it in the disciple's ear, he does it in a particular way so as to emphasize certain sounds – something which is not known to all. As a matter of fact there are various phonetic variations of 'Rama' that have different effects.

The story of the sage Valmiki is well-known, but it has now lost its true significance and so seems rather childish. It is said that Valmiki was illiterate and a mere rustic. His master told him to repeat the mantra 'Rama, Rama' – but after some time he forgot and started chanting it in reverse, '*Mara, mara*' – and he became enlightened!

When the real keys with which to unravel such mysteries are lost, all sorts of troubles arise. The fact is that while chanting the mantra 'Rama, Rama' after a period of time you automatically begin to chant '*Mara, mara*'; so creating a circuit. When 'Rama, Rama' is chanted quickly, the chanting turns into 'Mara, mara' – then it has the right phonetic emphasis. Then something unique happens: you cease to be, you are no more, and in that very moment when you cease to be or you die to your identity, the mantra becomes complete. That is the moment of real experience – when you have ceased, your ego has died.

It is interesting to note that if this process is completed properly you will begin with the repetition of 'Rama, Rama,' and very soon a moment will arise when you will be repeating '*Mara, mara*' instead. Even if you want to say 'Rama' you will not be able to, your whole being will be repeating '*Mara, mara*.' At that moment you will die to yourself – and that is the first step of meditation. When your dying to yourself is total, you will suddenly find that '*Mara, mara*' is beginning to revert back to 'Rama, Rama'. And when 'Rama, Rama' begins from within you, without your doing it, you will actually experience Rama, the ultimate reality – but not before that. In between, the transformation to *Mara* is essential.

So there are three parts to the mantra: begin with Rama; lose your identity in *Mara* and then the mantra will evolve into Rama. The second step of *Mara* is a necessary part of the process: unless that happens in the middle, the real, ultimate Rama experience in the third step will not happen. If you know the true phonetics and if you chant it properly – if you put the stress on *ra* and less on *ma*, only then will 'Rama' change into *Mara*. When *ma* has less emphasis, it becomes like a valley, and *ra* becomes the peak, the highest peak. In your repeating the *ma* of 'Rama' with less emphasis, the transformation happens, and very soon you will find that *ma* becomes the peak and *ra* becomes the valley. Then you are repeating *Mara, mara* – 'Death, death' – without your knowing it.

Like waves in the ocean, after every peak there is a valley. Like waves in the ocean, sound also has waves – like a crescendo and diminuendo in music. Unless you are aware of the proper phonetic pronunciation, you can go on repeating a mantra but it will produce no results.

Whoever wrote this story – that Valmiki repeated *Mara, mara* because he was illiterate and an ignorant rustic – is far from the truth. Valmiki *was* illiterate and a rustic, but in this particular instance he was an adept. He knew the science of how to chant 'Rama' in order to transform the sound into *Mara*. Only after this intervening transformation is 'Rama' born. And this 'Rama' will not be the one spoken by you because during that second step of *Mara* you cease to be. Then who will be repeating it? The real 'Rama' that is born within you at the end of the second step will not be spoken by you but will be just a happening, in spite of you. It will happen automatically, it will not be your repetition.

The value of the *shrutis*, the scriptures that are heard or listened to, is the phonetic emphasis. Only a person who knows the science of phonetics can pass on the knowledge of *shruti*; only then they will be useful. Otherwise, the words will be the same as those written in the book – anybody can read them – but the science will remain unknown. This science of sound – its ascents and descents, and the lengths of soundless intervals – constitutes the whole mystery.

There used to be a complete scripture of mantras, and temples served as the laboratories where they were being tested. For the seeker this was their inner value and meaning. The number of people experiencing self-realization within the precincts of a temple has always been greater than of those who have experienced it outside the temple. This has happened in spite of the fact that the divine is as much present outside the temples as inside. Today this experience is not happening even inside the temples.

People like Mahavira, who had to experiment without the use of temples, had to find different methods, more painstaking than the ones used inside the temples. Mahavira had to spend years mastering many different types of postures, so that he could create the circuit of energy within. He did not want to use the help of the temple – but the alternative was a lengthy process of difficult practices which took years, and which could only be accomplished by a man with the iron will of Mahavira.

Buddha also attained enlightenment without the help of the temple. But soon after the deaths of both Mahavira and Buddha, temples had to be constructed because what a temple could offer the ordinary man was not given by either Buddha or Mahavira – the practice which Buddha and Mahavira advocated was not always possible for the ordinary man to achieve.

Today, if we can fully understand the science of sound circuits we can invent even better instruments than these temples. Research in this direction is at present already going on, and it will be possible to invent better instruments because now we know a lot about electricity. But such experiments can be dangerous too. Still, if scientific arrangements are properly set up, whatever help a temple once gave will be available through scientific technology – because the circle of energy that was once created in the temple could be created by some other method. Then you could keep a small instrument in your pocket to activate the electrical circuit within you, and on that electronic instrument you might even be able to store sounds recorded to create circuits within you.

Research is presently being done in this area in America. Seven or eight scientists in America are now engaged in a fascinating study, aimed at showing that all our experiences of pleasure and pain are nothing but electrical currents passing through certain centers of the body.

For example, if your body is pricked all over with a needle, at some of those points you will not experience pain. There are a few dead spots in your body where you will not feel anything. If someone pricks your back in a dozen or so places, three or four of those places will have no sensation. In exactly the same way, there will be some five to ten points of great sensitivity, where even the slightest pricking will cause a lot of pain.

Our head has many sensitive spots. There are millions of cells in the brain, and each one has a particular sensitivity. When you say you feel happy, electricity is flowing through one particular center, giving you a sense of happiness. Suppose you are sitting next to your beloved, holding her hand, and you say you are feeling happy – what is happening? If a scientist described this phenomenon, he would say that electricity is flowing through a particular center in your brain, and that it is only your past mental association with this person that makes you so happy in her presence. But you may no longer feel that happiness after two or three months because if you use a certain center very often, letting electricity flow through it frequently, that center becomes insensitive.

For example, if you repeatedly prick your foot at a particular point with a needle, the pain will become less and less. Tomorrow the pain will be less than today, and the day after that it will be even less. If you go on doing it, this point will develop a callous which will become insensitive and will not feel any pain at all. People who play the sitar develop insensitive surface skin on their fingers, and then any amount of plucking on the instrument's strings does not make any difference – their fingers don't feel any pain.

So if after three or four months you feel that your love has died, or become less, it does not mean that your love was fragile, it only means that the point within you from where the feeling of happiness was coming has become desensitized because of frequent use. If your beloved goes away for three or four months, when she returns she can make you feel happy again.

Scientists' experiments on rats have been very revealing. The brain of a rat was opened up, and a 'window' kept open through which to observe what happens when a rat is having sexual intercourse. The particular point through which the electric current was passing when the rat ejaculated was noted. After that, this point was connected to an electrode and the 'window' was closed. The other end of the electrode was connected to a machine which could release a controlled amount of electricity. There was a switch which could be operated by pressing it, which would release electricity – the same intensity of electricity that was flowing at the time of the rat's ejaculation.

The rat was taught how to operate the switch, and whenever it pressed it, the required amount of electricity was released by the machine, and that activated the point in the brain connected at the other end of the wire, giving the rat the same pleasure as in sexual intercourse. The rat felt very happy when it pressed the switch – it was so happy that it began to press the switch again and again. You will be surprised to know that the rat did not do anything else after that for the next twenty-four hours. It simply went on pushing the button – six thousand times within an hour! It did not bother to eat, drink or sleep, but just kept pressing the switch until finally it collapsed, exhausted.

The scientist who was doing the experiment said that the rat enjoyed the pleasure of sex so much – more than it had ever done through intercourse – although it was not actually having intercourse but only experiencing sexual pleasure because of the electrical current released in its brain. The scientist claimed that very soon that same sensation would lose its charm for the rat and become very ordinary.

The day we are able to connect the human brain to an electrode to receive the right electrical current at the right point, we will not be able to find anyone who will actually want to take part in sex – because there is practically no gain, and a lot of energy is lost. Instead one can carry a small battery-operated device in one's pocket, and whenever one wants to, one can activate the sex center and experience the same joy as in sexual intercourse. But this has its own dangers.

Once it is possible to locate the various centers in the brain, such as for doubt or for anger, these centers can be surgically removed. The center connected with rebelliousness can be disconnected and man will become very docile. However, governments can misuse such scientific achievements.

Scientists are not aware of it, yet it may be that with the help of scientific instruments we can provide a milieu like that which exists in a temple. The experiences – which took hours, months, and years to obtain with sound effects in a temple – may be more easily created with scientific instruments. So what I am saying is: the temple was based on very scientific foundations;

through the medium of sound, feelings of happiness, peace, love, and bliss were aroused. And in the presence of these feelings, one's whole attitude toward life could be transformed.

On the other hand, what science can do may be fraught with great dangers. The main danger lies in the fact that whatever science does becomes technological, and consciousness does not play a part in it. It may be possible to bring about the same state as is possible through being in a temple, by means of electrical instruments, but then a real transformation of consciousness will not be possible. The heights of consciousness and transformation cannot happen that way; what a man can get by pressing a switch will not bring about any fundamental transformation. So I do not see any possibility of such instruments fulfilling the need for temples.

You may wonder if temples can be used today in these changed times. Yes, it is possible, but the conventional orthodox priest who is in the temple today will not be able to explain what was happening, and how it was happening, in the temples in ancient times. He still has the key, but he does not have any idea of the hidden mysteries behind it. The whole philosophy and science of the temples can still be of use today. And we can create better temples now because we have better building materials. We can set up a whole sound system in such a way that sound can be magnified a thousandfold. Walls can be made that are so sensitive that if you chant the mantra 'Om' once, the walls will echo it thousands of times. Today we have better instruments, but we should know the key which can unlock the secrets of our being.

In the old days, there had to be at least one door in a temple, but now we can build a temple without any doors. In the old days, the people who built the temples were generally living in houses like huts, made of cow-dung and clay. They did the best they could within their limitations, and what they did was great. Today we have wonderful technological skills, but we are not able to benefit from them.

So far we have been discussing the benefit of temples for those who entered them. But temples have their external significance and utility as well. We have discussed how meditators enter a temple, and go deep into meditation and prayer. But even a person just passing near a temple was benefited, although now that does not happen anymore. Today even those who go inside come out with nothing. But in those days the temple could even help a person who had just been near it, because the people who were inside the temple were really doing something. Hundreds of meditators in the temple were activating special sound vibrations, by which the whole atmosphere of the temple became charged. The temple was not just vibrating within; it was also vibrating outside, and spreading subtle waves outside as well. The whole environment became alive because the temple itself was alive.

This was the significance of a 'living temple.' A 'living statue' signified the same thing – they affected even those who had not come there for any particular benefit. A temple could only be called a living temple if someone could pass by it casually and suddenly sense that the air had changed, the atmosphere transformed – even though he may not have known that there was a temple in the vicinity.

Suppose you are walking along a road on a dark night: you are passing by a temple when suddenly you experience some change within; you were thinking of doing something wrong and suddenly your thoughts change. You were thinking of killing someone and suddenly you feel full of compassion. But all this can only happen if the temple is charged, where every brick and stone of the temple, the doors and gates, are all charged. Then the whole temple will have become a temple of living vibrations.

A unique method is used to charge the bell that hangs in front of the temples. Whoever enters rings the bell does it with total consciousness, not with a sleepy mind. When you ring the bell of a temple – not half asleep but with alertness – that creates a discontinuity in your thoughts, a sort of break in the chain of your thoughts, and you become aware of a changed atmosphere. There is a similarity between the sound of the bell and the sound of 'Om' – in fact there is some inner relationship. The sound of the bell continues charging the temple all day long, and the sound of 'Om' also charges the temple with its vibrations.

Many other things like that were made use of in the temple; they had their inner connections. It might be an earthen lamp filled with ghee, the burning of incense, the use of sandalwood paste, or flowers, or any other fragrance – all were related. It was not a question of a particular deity liking a specific flower; it was a question of the harmony of the temple. What type of sound and what type of fragrance was harmonious with the temple was decided through experience. Only a certain flower with a certain fragrance, which blended harmoniously with a certain sound, was used; others with different fragrances were prohibited.

In a mosque, only *lobhan*, a kind of fragrant resin could be used as incense, and in a temple, only *dhoop* and *agarbatti* fragrances. All these had their connections with sound. With the sound of 'Allah' there is an inner harmony with the fragrance of *lobhan*. These links or connections were all discovered through the inner search for the ultimate; they were not found through any thinking process. I will tell you how this was done.

You may sit in a room where no *lobhan* has been burned and repeat, 'Allah' – not just 'Allah' but *Allahoo*, with a special emphasis on *Hoo*. You will find that slowly, slowly this 'Allah' sound disappears and automatically only *Hoo* will go on being repeated. When this happens, you will suddenly find that your whole room is fragrant with the smell of *lobhan*. It was discovered that *lobhan* is similar to a substance that emanates from you. So, *lobhan* is burned in mosques with a view to helping people repeat the mantra, *Hoo*. Then the process is twofold: the emanation of the fragrance from within a person may take some time, but the same fragrance can initially be provided outwardly in the mosque. However, the repetition of 'Om' can never bring about the fragrance of *lobhan*. This sound strikes another center which cannot produce that fragrance.

There are separate areas of fragrance within our body, and these are linked with our thoughts and feelings. That is why Jainas believe that Mahavira's body never gave out any bad odor – his body had a certain fragrance on the basis of which it was possible to recognize a tirthankara, a Jaina enlightened master. In Mahavira's time, eight other people claimed to be tirthankaras, but this particular fragrance was not coming from them. None of them was less knowledgeable than Mahavira; they were of the same spiritual stature, but they were not practitioners of that system of spiritual discipline which produces this fragrance – so their claims were rejected.

Buddha was in no way inferior to Mahavira. He was of the same caliber and state of consciousness as Mahavira, but because he was not following the same method as Mahavira, his body could not emit the same fragrance. This fragrance had also emanated from Parshwanath, a tirthankara who had died long before Mahavira's time. His contemporaries were still living, and they confirmed that Mahavira's fragrance was similar to Parshwanath's. The ultimate result of a certain mantra process was this particular fragrance.

This was a memory-based arrangement for determining the authenticity of a tirthankara. So though Mahavira never claimed he was a tirthankara, he was readily proclaimed to be one. Makkhali Goshal, on the other hand, did make the claim but could not prove it. You may wonder why fragrance was used as the criterion: the test had to be that deep and infallible – words cannot be relied upon. The whole individuality of the person had to emit the special fragrance that would indicate that a certain flowering had happened within him, that the culmination of the mantra process which gives birth to a tirthankara had happened.

Makkhali Goshal, Ajit Keshkambal, and Sanjay Vilethiputra were all claimants, very knowledgeable, of equal caliber to Mahavira – each of them had thousands of followers who claimed that their master was a tirthankara – but they all disappeared into oblivion. On the other hand, Mahavira was absolutely silent on this point and never made any claim, but in the end it was decided that only the person whose body emitted that particular fragrance could be a tirthankara.

Every mantra creates its own fragrance. Those who have practiced chanting 'Om' have known a certain fragrance. Similarly, every mantra produces a particular type of inner light. How much light should be provided in a temple was decided on the basis of that inner light – neither more nor less. The ignorance of those who sit under dazzling electric lights in temples is simply amazing: it is not needed at all because only as much light is needed as is within the inner sky – a very soft and inoffensive light. So a ghee lamp was used because it is not at all offensive and does not dazzle the eyes.

It may not be easy to understand the difference between a kerosene light and the ghee light if you have never experimented with meditating on light. Light a lamp filled with kerosene oil and concentrate on the flame for one hour: your eyes will start burning and will become tired and painful. Then light another lamp with ghee in it, and concentrate on that flame for one hour: your eyes will feel cooler and soothed. All these things were revealed by the inner experiences of thousands of people, and parallels were found that became external aids. Of course, it is not possible to provide a lamp exactly the same as the inner light, so only the most approximate was found. The exact fragrance which is produced within you after chanting a particular mantra cannot be found outside, so we have to be content with the nearest approximation.

Sandalwood paste became popular in all the temples. The place on the forehead where the sandalwood paste is applied is called the *agya* chakra in Yoga. Practicing certain mantras produces an inner experience of sandalwood perfume, but the source of that fragrance is the *agya* chakra. Whenever the third eye experience intensifies, a sandalwood perfume emanates – so sandalwood perfume has become symbolic of that experience, hence we apply sandalwood paste to the forehead. When the *agya* chakra emanates this fragrance a sort of coolness is felt, as if you have put a piece of ice on the third eye. There is a difference between cooling things and soothing things – just the same as there is between a kerosene oil lamp and a lamp filled with ghee.

Ice is cooling, but it is not balmy or soothing. The cooling sensation of ice lasts only a short while and is followed by a feeling of heat. Ice is certainly cold, but not soothing or balmy. Eventually the feeling is bound to be that of heat; you feel a little hotter than before. But sandalwood paste is balmy and not cold; it only soothes. The coolness has a kind of depth. If ice is put on the *agya* chakra it will only make the surface cold. If sandalwood is applied to the *agya* chakra, you will feel that its soothing effect is seeping into deeper layers beyond the skin. The coolness has to penetrate to where the third eye is. Those who experienced the working of the *agya* chakra and felt its balmy effect looked for a parallel and found it in sandalwood paste. It has the same fragrance as that which emanates from within.

All these external aids are just parallels. And when a temple has been provided with them, it becomes charged. So there is a stipulation that no one should go to a temple without first taking a bath – taking a cold bath breaks one's mechanicalness and thought associations. Nobody was allowed to enter the temple without ringing the bell, and nobody was to go into the temple in old or dirty clothes. In fact silk clothes had to be worn when visiting a temple because silk helps to generate body electricity and to protect it – so silk clothes always remain new, however much you wear them.

The temple became charged by all these precautions and arrangements, and so also anyone just passing by was affected by the magnetic field of the temple.

It is said about Mahavira that within a certain radius around him – wherever he might be – it was impossible to commit any violence. It was his charged field, within which no violence was possible. He was like a walking temple, and within that sphere anything happening would suddenly be changed – it was a noosphere effect.

Teilhard de Chardin has coined a new word, *noosphere*, in place of *atmosphere*. *Atmosphere* means the external climate. *Noosphere* means the mental or psychological climate, and within that field, certain types of happenings do not take place at all.

In ancient days, forest ashrams were run by sages. The surrounding atmosphere of an ashram was considered pure, inviolable. If anything wrong happened among the disciples, the sage punished himself – not them – because it meant that the field had lost its essential quality. So the disciples could not be blamed: to reprimand them was futile. Some untoward event only meant that the field had lost its sanctity, so the master himself would repent, undergo a fast, and purify himself.

But Gandhi misunderstood this idea. Self-purification was not meant to be a way to reprove anyone else; it was not intended to put pressure on another person. The idea was not to torture oneself or to go fasting unto death in order to change someone else's heart or conscience. Gandhi did not understand this. The sage was not purifying himself to change somebody else, he was doing it to recharge his field and the surrounding area. If this field is transformed, if the mental climate is transformed, the man living within it will also become transformed. There was no question of changing someone's conscience but of changing the surroundings and the magnetic field around oneself.

Every realized person utilizes this kind of a field of influence. People like Mahavira were like walking temples. Such people could not be expected to stay permanently in one particular place. So something else, more stable, was needed that could become the center of life for a whole town – something around which the lives of people would go on being transformed.

We needed a place, a temple, where we could make our daily offerings and receive something in return. We may not even have been aware of what was happening; everything happened by itself. Anyone passing the temple received something invaluable. There was a huge magnetic field created around it, and just as an iron filing attracted by a magnet is caught in its magnetic field, so anyone passing by the temple would be attracted and influenced by its energy – the field of a temple was like that.

It is said about Moses that when he went to the mountain, he saw a divine fire burning there. A whole bush was burning – but in the middle of it there were flowers in full bloom and green leaves. Moses had set out in search for God. As he stepped toward the bush, suddenly he heard a voice coming from it, saying, 'You foolish man! Leave your shoes outside this place!'

There was no demarcation line, so Moses continued walking, looking for the threshold where he could leave his shoes. When he crossed a certain point where he felt a change, where he felt something within him change – an inner transformation – that was where he left his shoes. This was the threshold of the energy field. He entered it and prayed for forgiveness for desecrating this sacred place.

A temple had a charged field around it that was very vibrant, and that field had a helpful influence on the entire village. This is not a fiction, results were actually achieved. The characteristic simplicity, innocence, and purity of Indian villages for thousands of years, were more due to the charged field of the temples than to the villages themselves. However poor a village, the existence of a temple was an absolutely necessity. Without a temple everything seemed chaotic, without a rhythm.

For thousands of years, villages maintained a sort of sacredness, and there were great, invisible sources of that sacredness. The worst thing which could be done to destroy Eastern culture was to destroy this charged field of the temples. With the destruction of those vibrant temples, the entire Eastern culture crumbled.

That is why people are skeptical about the value of temples today. Whoever has gone to school or college, and has been taught only language and logic – only developing the intellect, the heart remaining closed – has never experienced a living temple and does not see any meaning in one. So temples have slowly lost their significance.

India cannot be India again until the temples again become alive. The whole alchemy of India lay in her temples; India received everything through her temples. There was a time when everything that happened in the life of a person revolved around the temple. If he was sick he went to the temple; if he was unhappy he ran to the temple; even if he was happy he ran to the temple to give thanks. If something good happened in the family, he went to the temple with fruit and flowers; if there were problems he would go to the temple to pray. For him the temple was all and everything. All his hopes, longings, and aspirations revolved around the temple. However poor he was, he kept the temple decorated with gold and silver and all sorts of jewels.

Today when people are dying of hunger, all that extravagance for the temple looks like madness: 'Remove the temples! Build a hospital, or open a school, let the temples be opened up for the homeless, let them be used!' Temples have become useless because we have forgotten their real use. We think, 'Why should there be gold and silver and jewels lying in the temples when people are starving to death?'

But it is worth remembering that those same hungry people gave the gold and diamonds to the temples. Whatsoever they felt was most valuable to them they gave to the temple – because whatsoever they had known of great value in their life they had learned from the temple. There was nothing that could sufficiently repay their debt, so they gave whatever they had. And there were good reasons to do so – nothing continues for thousands of years without good reasons. The invisible fruit of the temple's influence were continuously being received; there were clear and apparent benefits in being near a temple.

Man always forgets. Whatever is sublime and valuable we forget; whatever is trivial and commonplace we remember continuously, twenty-four hours a day. We have to make an effort to remember God, but our desires and passions don't need to be remembered, they are there all the time. Going downhill is easy; going uphill is always difficult.

So the temple was built in the center of the village, so that during the day one could go there as frequently as needed – it kept the search alive. Very few of us are naturally inspired to seek; most of us only feel inspired when we actually see things. When there were no airplanes, we did not have any desire to travel by plane. Yes, people like the Wright brothers did dream of flying – they invented the airplane – but the ordinary person will not have such dreams unless he sees an plane.

So when we could see godliness personified within the shape of a temple, something of godliness lingered on in our minds. This was especially so for people who could not visualize the unmanifest divine. For those who could, there was no need for a temple. But in a way, those people caused great harm to the temple because they said that the temples had no use and should be dispensed with. I myself used to say, 'Temples are useless, remove them!'

But slowly I began to realize that if the temples were destroyed, how would those who cannot visualize the unmanifest form of godliness, ever be able to even think of godliness? From that angle, sometimes difficulties do arise. If a person like Mahavira – who never needed a temple – speaks from his level of consciousness, he may want the temples removed, but if he thinks about your need he will stop saying this.

The temple remains a source of inspiration all twenty-four hours of your day. You remember that there is one more door in life: other than your shop or house, apart from your wife and your wealth, a dimension which is neither a part of the marketplace nor of your desires. It gives you neither wealth nor fame, nor does it satisfy your desires – the temple is a constant reminder of that. There are moments in life when you are tired of the marketplace, bored with your family – these are the moments when you can find harmony in the temple.

If the temple is destroyed then there is no other alternative. If you are tired of the food at home, you can go to a hotel or restaurant but if you are tired of the marketplace, where will you go? The temple provides a different dimension, away from the world of give and take. So those who made temples to be like the marketplace have destroyed them.

A temple is not a place for bargaining, it is a place for rest and relaxation where, tired and exhausted from all your worldly activities, you can find relief and peace. There are no conditions for entering a temple: 'You can only come if you have this much money, you can only come if you have this much knowledgeability' or 'You can only come if you have this much prestige' – a temple accepts you as you are. It is a place so simple that you are accepted as you are.

You have become tired of the kind of life you are living many times. At such times you may have felt the door to prayer opening. If this door has opened even once, it can open again and again, even in your shop and your home. Whenever you want to, at any time, this door will be easy for you to reach – because the moments that can be called truly great rarely come. It is not necessary to go on a pilgrimage or in search of a Mahavira or a Buddha – such moments are too short-lived. There should be some place just nearby, which you can simply enter.

Childhood memories are very important. Scientists say that by the age of seven a child has learned almost all the fundamentals on which the superstructure of his knowledge will be built. Very little that is new will be added, but all his knowledge will be built on that base. If we are not able to form an association with the temple in the child's mind by the time he is seven, then it becomes difficult, even impossible, to do so later. A lot of effort will be needed and then too it will only be superficial.

That is why we wanted the temple to be the child's first memory after birth. His surroundings were planned in such a way he would grow up near the temple, gradually coming to know it and absorbing it into his life. The temple would become an integral part of his being, and when he entered worldly life, the temple would have its own special place inside him – because it was the temple which would finally provide a retreat for him during the mature years of his life. So we wanted the temple to have a place in his mind right from birth – later on it would become difficult.

All those who lived within the vicinity of the temple had an impression of it imprinted on their minds. It went so deep into their unconscious it was no longer an idea but became a part of their being. So all over the world the forms and shapes of temples may have differed, but the temple itself was indispensable.

In the world which is evolving now, the temple is not considered indispensable, other things have taken its place: schools, hospitals, and libraries. But they relate only to the material, they have no connection at all with the beyond. Something else is needed that points to the transcendental. When we get up in the morning, we should be hearing temple bells ringing; and when we go to sleep at night, we should be hearing religious songs from the temple.

There was an incident in Mahavira's life . . .

A thief was lying on his deathbed, and his son asked him for a final word of advice that would help him in his work. The thief said, 'Don't have anything to do with a person called Mahavira. If you know he is in your village, run to the next. If he is passing your way on the road, hide somewhere in a side street. And if without realizing it you are somewhere you can hear his words, immediately close your eyes and ears. Above all, beware of him!'

When the son asked him why he should be so afraid of Mahavira, his father told him not to argue: 'Just listen to what I say. If you go near that man, our business will be in danger and the family will starve.'

What happened next is very interesting. The thief's son always avoided Mahavira, but one day he made a mistake. Mahavira was sitting silently in a mango grove, and unknowingly the thief's son happened to pass that way. Suddenly Mahavira started speaking. The thief heard half the sentence, closed his ears, and ran. But he had already heard half the sentence, and that landed him in a lot of trouble. He was being chased by the police – all the state police were after him for his thieving – and some weeks later he was eventually caught.

Thieving was in his family and he was an expert in his trade. He was so clever he never left behind any incriminating evidence. It was well-known he was a thief and had committed a lot of thefts; everybody knew about it, but there was no evidence. So there was no alternative but to make him confess.

He was made totally drunk, and kept in such a state of intoxication he remained unconscious for two or three days. When he did open his eyes again, he was still in a state of semi-consciousness. All around him he saw beautiful women standing, and he asked where he was. He was told he had died, and that preparations were being made to take him to either heaven or hell. He was told people were waiting for him to become conscious, so he could confess the sins he had committed. If he did, he would be taken to heaven, otherwise he would be sent to hell. But if he spoke the truth he would be saved.

He now felt he should tell the truth and so not lose the chance of going to heaven – now he had died, there was nothing to fear. But just at that moment he remembered the half-sentence he had heard Mahavira say. Mahavira had been talking about gods and ghosts. He had also mentioned the *yamadoots*, who take people to the worlds beyond death. The thief had heard him say the toes of *yamadoots* are always inverted. Opening his eyes, he saw that the feet of the people standing by him were normal, so he became alert. He now saw there was no need to confess. He saw through the trick and told them he had not committed any sins – what could he confess?

If they wanted, they could take him to hell. But as he had not committed any sins, how could they? So they had to let him go.

Then he went running to Mahavira, fell at his feet, and asked him to complete the sentence which had saved him. When half of Mahavira's sentence had saved him, of how much more benefit would be the whole sentence! He told Mahavira he was totally surrendered to him.

Sometime or other he was bound to be caught and hanged, but if he heard the rest of the sentence he might still be saved – that is why Mahavira used to say that if even half the sentence of an awakened one is heard, it might be useful one day. Similarly, a man running past a temple, or just casually passing by, hearing the sound vibrations coming from a temple or smelling the fragrance of the place – even that can be of help to him.

2
The Alchemy of Places of Pilgrimage

In the Pacific Ocean there is a small island, Easter Island, on which there are one thousand huge stone statues, all about twenty feet tall. The population of the island is now just two hundred. When the island was first discovered, it was found that it was so small it could not produce food for more than two hundred people – which suggests that its population could never have been greater. When only two hundred people can live there, it was surprising to find such huge stone statues, and as many as one thousand! Five statues for every person! And those people would not have been able to make such huge statues even if they had wanted to because their lives were spent in taking care of their daily needs. What could be the purpose of those statues? Who would have made them and why? Many such questions arose for the historians.

In central Asia there is another place equally puzzling. It could have been meant for use as an airport but since airplanes had not yet been invented, this hypothesis was not possible. The area seemed to have been developed fifteen to twenty thousand years ago. And only after the airplane had been invented was it thought this place in central Asia might once have served as an airport.

I am telling you these things to convey to you the idea: we will not be able to understand the significance of these places of pilgrimage until we ourselves realize the need for them.

When the statues of Easter Island were photographed from the air, one could imagine they had been erected at certain geometrical points, in such a way they might be seen from the moon on particular nights. Those who have studied this subject think that we in this century are not the first people to look for life on other planets. Many times before, experiments and attempts have been made to find living beings and other forms of life on other planets, so communication could be established with them. And many coded systems were created to make it possible for any other living beings to contact the earth.

These twenty-foot-high statues are not meaningful in themselves, but when their whole pattern is observed from the air, there are indications of some signs and secret messages. Those signs could only be read from the moon: as long as we had not seen the statues from the air, we could not imagine what use they might have – they were still just statues. In the same way, there are many things on this earth about which we will know nothing until our civilization rediscovers them, and sets up a similar situation again.

Just three or four days ago, I was talking about a small iron box which was found in Teheran. It was kept in the British Museum for a long time, and for many years was just lying there. It has now been found to be a kind of battery which was used in Teheran about two thousand years ago! It was beyond anyone's imagination that such a battery should exist in Teheran two thousand years ago, but now it is an established fact that it is a battery. If we had not already invented the storage battery, we would never have been able to imagine such a box might be a battery. The very idea, the very concept, would not have arisen in us.

A *tirtha* – a sacred place of pilgrimage – is a unique invention, very deep and symbolic, created by an ancient civilization, but our present civilization has lost all knowledge of the significance of such places. Today visiting a place of pilgrimage is just a dead ritual for us. We simply tolerate them, without knowing why places of pilgrimage were established, what their use was, and who made them.

What can be seen on the surface is not everything; there are hidden meanings which are not visible from the outside.

Firstly we need to realize that the purpose and meaning of the sacred place of pilgrimage has become lost to our civilization, and so today people who go on a pilgrimage are wasting their time. Those who oppose the idea are also wasting their time – however right they seem to be – because they know nothing about such places. Neither the people who visit the places of pilgrimage, nor those who oppose the idea, know their purpose – so let us try to understand a few things about them.

There is a famous place of pilgrimage for Jainas known as Samved Shikhar. Twenty-two out of the twenty-four tirthankaras of the Jainas have died there, have left their bodies there. It all seems to have been prearranged: otherwise it is impossible that, out of twenty-four, twenty-two should have happened to die in the same place, with long periods of time in between them. If we believe the Jainas, there is a gap of one hundred thousand years between the first and the twenty-fourth tirthankara – that twenty-two of them died in the same place is worth thinking about.

The place of pilgrimage for Mohammedans is the Kaaba. Until the time of Mohammed, there were three hundred and sixty-five statues in Kaaba – a different idol for each day of the year. All these statues were removed or destroyed, but the central stone which was the center of the temple was not removed. The Kaaba is much more ancient than the Mohammedan religion: the history of Islam is only about fourteen hundred years old, but that black stone in the Kaaba is hundreds of thousands of years old.

Another interesting fact is that the stone does not seem to belong to our earth. How did it come to earth? The only hypothesis we have is that it is part of a meteor. Whenever a meteor disintegrates, thousands of stone fragments fall toward the earth. Many of these are burned up before they reach the earth. At night when we see stars falling, these are not stars, but meteors. Sometimes even huge stones manage to reach the earth. These stones are of a different composition from those on the earth, and the stone at Kaaba is such a stone.

But there are people who have gone deeper into this, who feel that such big stones could have been brought to earth and left here, just as our astronauts have left a few things from the earth on the moon. Whatever the astronauts have left on the moon will safely remain there, even if there is a nuclear war and life on this earth is destroyed. And if ever some civilization reaches the moon, they will be very surprised to see the things we have left there.

So the stone at Kaaba may not be part of a meteorite, but may have been left by the inhabitants of another planet. Perhaps it was once possible to communicate with them through the medium of this stone, but now only its worship has remained. The science of how it might have been used as a means of communication has been lost.

An unmanned Russian spaceship became lost when its radio contact with the earth was broken, so it was no longer possible to trace it. Whether it was burned up, destroyed, or is still somewhere in space is not known, but if it has landed on some planet, and if the inhabitants of that planet were able to repair the radio, they could re-establish contact with the earth. They might also demolish it, or store it in their museum! They may even be afraid and in awe of it – or they may even start worshipping it. The Kaaba stone may be an instrument sent out by spacemen from some other planet to establish contact with the earth.

I am telling you this only by way of illustration, to explain that a sacred place of pilgrimage was once a medium to establish contact – not with living beings in space, but with enlightened souls who had lived on this earth.

A very deep and intense experiment was made on Samved Shikhar by the twenty-two tirthankaras just as they were leaving their bodies. On that mountain they tried to intensify and multiply the vibrations of their developed consciousness so that it would be easier for us to communicate with them. It was thought that if so many souls of such consciousness left their body from the same place, a path between that place and another plane could be laid – and such a path *has* existed.

The rainfall is not the same everywhere on earth: there are some areas of heavy rain, where it rains as much as five hundred inches a year, and desert areas where there is no rain or it is very scarce. Similarly, there are places which are very cold, where there is nothing but snow everywhere; and there are areas so hot it is difficult to make ice. In the same way on the earth there are places with high-density consciousness and low-density consciousness. Conscious attempts have been made to create areas of high consciousness, fields charged with human consciousness. They do not happen automatically, but are a result of the consciousnesses of powerful individuals.

Twenty-two tirthankaras traveling to that one mountain, entering samadhi and leaving their bodies there, created – in some special sense – a highly-charged field of consciousness at Samved Shikhar. It was intended that if someone sits there, chanting the special mantras given by those twenty-two tirthankaras, his journey into out-of-the-body experiences would immediately begin. This is as scientific an experiment as any which takes place in a laboratory.

The only reason for creating the places of pilgrimage was to experiment with creating powerfully charged fields of conscious energies, so that anyone could easily begin his inner journey.

There are two methods of making a boat move: one method is to open the sails at the right time, in the direction of the wind, and not to use the oars; the other method is not to open the sails, but to help the boat move with the use of the oars. The places of pilgrimage are places where the stream of consciousness is flowing automatically: you just have to stand in the middle of the stream with the sails of your consciousness open, and you begin your journey onward. You will be able to travel far more easily and faster in such places than anywhere else – and alone. Elsewhere, you may unknowingly reach some negative place, and open up your sails in the wrong direction: you may move further away from your destination and become lost.

For example, if you are sitting in meditation in a place full of negative emotions – where butchers are killing animals the whole day – there will be a great struggle and conflict in your mind. In meditation you become very receptive, open and vulnerable, so whatever is happening around you at that time enters you. So when you meditate it is always necessary to choose a place which will not take you in a wrong direction. Whenever you have disturbing thoughts during meditation, or find it difficult to be silent, move from such a place. One can sit in meditation even in a jail, but that requires a very strong individuality. Different methods are required to help you meditate in a jail: you have to create a line of demarcation over which negative forces cannot enter.

But in a *tirtha*, a sacred place of pilgrimage, such a line is not necessary: in such a place you require a technique that helps you to drop all resistance and to open your doors and windows from all sides. There, positive energy is flowing in abundance. Hundreds of people have traveled into the unknown from there and have created a path. Yes, it should be called a path – it is as if they have made a path by cutting down trees and removing bushes blocking the way, so that those walking behind them find it easier to travel. On the religious path, efforts are made by the higher, stronger consciousnesses to help weaker people in every way. The place of pilgrimage was one such great experiment.

A place of pilgrimage is where currents flow from the body toward the soul, where the whole atmosphere is charged; where people have achieved samadhi, where for centuries people have been realizing their enlightenment. Such places have become especially charged. In such a place, if you just open your sails, without doing anything else, your journey will begin.

So, all religions have established their places of pilgrimage. Even those religions which were against temples have done it. It is surprising that religions that were against idol worship and temples established places of pilgrimage. It was easy to do without statues, but places of pilgrimage could not be done away with – because they have a value so vast that no religion could oppose or deny.

Jainas are not basically idol worshippers, nor are Mohammedans, Sikhs, or Buddhists – in the beginning Buddhists were not idol worshippers at all – but all of them have established their sacred places of pilgrimage. They had to. Without such places there is no meaning in a religion. If there were no such places, everything would have to be done by the individual, and in that case there would be no meaning or purpose to a religious commune.

The word *tirtha* means a sort of diving board from where one can jump into the infinite ocean. The Jaina word *tirthankara* means a creator of such a *tirtha*, such a place of pilgrimage. A person can only be called a *tirthankara* if he has charged an area into which ordinary people can enter, open themselves and begin their inner search. Jainas do not call them divine incarnations, but *tirthankaras*. A tirthankara is a greater phenomenon than a divine incarnation because if the divine enters a human form it is good, but if a man makes a place for others to enter the divine, it is a far higher event.

Jainism does not believe in a God, it believes in man's potential: that is why Jainas could benefit more deeply from the *tirtha* and the tirthankaras than the followers of any other religion. In the Jaina religion there is no concept of 'God's grace' or 'God's compassion' – Jainas do not think that God can give any help. The seeker is alone and has to travel by his own effort and energy.

But there are two ways in which he can then travel. On the first path, every man has to travel in his own boat, with the strength of his own hands, using the oars – one out of many may succeed – but on the second path, you can take the help of the winds and open up your sails, so you can travel faster and more easily.

But do such spiritual winds really exist? – yes, this is just what places of pilgrimage depend on. Is it possible, when a person like Mahavira is there, that a flow of energy toward some unknown dimension begins all around him? Can he create an energy flow toward a particular dimension, so that if someone enters this current he will be just carried along by it and will reach his ultimate destiny? – in fact, a sacred place of pilgrimage is a place with just this very flow.

On the earth there are physical signs of such places of pilgrimage, but, as time passes, these signs may disappear, so they have been highly protected by building temples or by erecting statues of those great seers. Great care has been taken for thousands of years that those places did not shift by even an inch from where the event had happened sometime in the past.

A search is going on even today for great treasures which have been hidden underground. For example, a search is going on for the richest treasure on earth – that of the last czar of Russia – which has been buried somewhere in America. It is certain such a treasure existed because the czar was only dethroned in 1917, not long ago. The exact location has been indicated on a map, but the description cannot be decoded. Similarly, the hidden treasures of the Gwalior king's family are somewhere in Gwalior. There is a map, but the exact location cannot be decoded – such maps are made in a secret code, so they do not fall into the wrong hands.

The locations of places of pilgrimage are similarly well indicated, but the exact place where the spiritual event occurred may not be known. Such places are hidden from the general public – this may surprise you. You may go to a place where it is said Mahavira reached nirvana, but there is a great possibility the exact spot is a little away from the place shown to everyone. The real location is shown only to those people who are authentic and deserving seekers. Ordinary people will bow down at the false place and return home. The real location will be kept hidden for those who come there out of an authentic spiritual search, and need that help for the jump.

There are many such places. In Arabia there is a small village called Alkufa where no outsider has been able to enter. We have gone to the moon, but no traveler has yet entered that small village. In fact up until now it has not been possible to locate this village. There is no doubt about its existence because history mentions it for thousands of years; history mentions it and there are also maps available. Its location is hidden for a special reason. When a Sufi reaches a deep state of consciousness during meditation he finds the key to the path; he is able to visualize the whole of Alkufa. Otherwise, whatever maps are available are false, to misguide people.

For the last three centuries many travelers from Europe have tried to reach Alkufa. Many of them died before they could return. Those who did come back did not reach the village, but had just been roaming around. One can reach it only through a special meditation, during which Alkufa becomes manifest. Once he sees the glimpse of the place in meditation, the Sufi meditator walks to it. Alkufa is a secret holy place, more ancient than Islam. The places of pilgrimage which are well-known, and can be visited by any pilgrim, are not the real ones – the real one is nearby, but hidden.

An interesting incident happened. When Vinoba Bhave, Gandhi's chief disciple, went to the Vishwanath temple in Varanasi with harijans, India's lowest caste, Karpatri – an orthodox brahmin scholar – said, 'You may enter, but now we shall have to make another temple because this one has been desecrated.'

And he actually began constructing another because to him the old temple had become useless. Superficially, Vinoba seems to be a more understanding person than Karpatri. Karpatri was very traditional, and ignorant of the modern world's trends and knowledge, but concerning the deep secret he was trying to support, he seems to be more knowledgeable.

The truth is that the Vishwanath temple is not the real one, and the one Karpatri wanted to have built instead of it would not be the real one either. The real temple is a third one which has to be kept hidden, otherwise any socio-religious reformer would desecrate it. The Vishwanath temple which is now standing has already been desecrated. There is no difficulty in desecrating a temple, you can if you want to. Any other temple being built there will also be false, but a false one will always have to be there, so the real one can remain hidden.

There are secret keys, mantras, through which one can enter Vishwanath temple, just as there are for Alkufa. Only occasionally some fortunate meditator has been able to enter. No ordinary householder has ever, or ever will be able to enter this temple. Not even all meditators gain entry – only the rare and fortunate ones. It is being kept hidden in every possible way. There are mantras through which its door will open, otherwise there is no way – there is no way to experience it, and there is no way to have any idea of it. Pilgrims go to the false temple, worship there and return to their homes, but over thousands of years this temple has also developed a sort of sanctity – even though it is false – because people have believed it to be the true one for so long.

All religions have tried not to allow people of other religions to enter their temples or places of pilgrimage. Why? The ones who made these rules knew of the dangers for such visitors. In a way, it is like a notice hanging on the entrance of an atomic energy laboratory, warning 'No entry except for atomic scientists.' We agree such restrictions are necessary – it is dangerous for non-scientists to enter – but when such restrictions are made in connection with a temple or place of pilgrimage we do not agree. We are not aware they also have their own science. These temples and places of pilgrimage are only meant for particular people.

It is like a conference of doctors standing around a patient discussing his disease. The patient listens to them, but cannot understand them because they are talking medical jargon, using Greek and Latin words. It is in the interest of the patient he should not understand. Similarly, all religions have developed their own code languages. They have their secret holy places, their secret languages, and secret scriptures. So what we understand to be places of pilgrimage are almost certainly not the right places. Such great traditions have to be preserved because if they fall into the wrong hands they may be misused. Ordinary people will only get into difficulties and will not benefit from them.

It is said that if you are allowed to enter the Sufi village of Alkufa you will go mad. It is said anyone entering accidentally will leave the village mad because Alkufa is created out of vibrations that cannot be tolerated by the ordinary mind. So it is better not to enter the town without the necessary preparation and discipline.

Understanding a few things about Alkufa will also help you to grasp things about other places of pilgrimage. It is said that it is not possible to sleep in Alkufa, so it is to be expected that those people who have not experimented deeply in staying awake will go mad.

The greatest accomplishment among Sufis is the night vigil: they keep awake the whole night. If a person does not eat for ninety days he will become very weak, but he will not die or go mad. An ordinary healthy man can easily fast for ninety days, but he cannot go without sleep for even twenty-one days. He can go without food for three months, but he cannot go without sleep for even three weeks. Three weeks is a very long time – it is difficult to go without sleep for even one week – but in Alkufa it is impossible to sleep at all.

A Buddhist monk was sent to me by someone from Sri Lanka. For three years this monk had not been able to sleep properly. The whole time his hands and feet were trembling, he was continuously perspiring, and he was very disturbed. He was afraid to even take one step – he had lost all confidence in himself. He was almost deranged. Strong tranquilizers could not help him sleep, only to lie down restlessly; inwardly he was still awake.

I asked him if he had ever practiced Buddha's *anapanasati* yoga – because for a Buddhist monk this practice is unavoidable. He said he did, so I told him he should give up the idea of getting any sleep because *anapanasati* yoga is a practice which makes sleep impossible. But it is only the initial step in the practice: once it is impossible to sleep, there is another step that must immediately be given. If you continue to do only the first part without this second step, you will become weak; you may even become mad and die.

Once sleep is destroyed from within, the quality of your consciousness changes so much that further progress can then be made. When I asked the monk if he knew the second phase of this practice, he said that no one had told him about it. The second part is not mentioned in any book, and writing about only the first part is dangerous because anyone who follows it will be unable to sleep. This was the reason why things were kept hidden, so they should not harm anyone. They were meant only to guide those who need help in their spiritual search.

This is why places of pilgrimages are necessary, but the real ones are kept hidden. And false places are created to keep you off the track until such a time when you are ready for the real one. No wrong person should reach the authentic place, but the right person will always find it.

Every place of pilgrimage has its own key. If you want to find the pilgrimage place of the Sufis, you will not be able to with the keys of the Jainas; and the Jaina places of pilgrimage cannot be found with the Sufi keys. Every religion has its own keys. I do not want to name it, but I shall tell you about the key of one place of pilgrimage.

The Tibetans have special mystical diagrams or yantras. These are keys. Hindus also have such instruments, thousands of them. In their houses, they write words like *labha shubha*, *prosperity*, and *goodness* – and they write some numbers underneath, without knowing why they are doing it. In their houses there may be such a yantra, which could be the key to a place of pilgrimage. They have no idea what they have written, but they go on doing it only because their forefathers were doing it.

Every outwardly created figure creates a figure within your consciousness. For example, if you keep staring at your window for a few minutes and then close your eyes, you will see a negative impression of the window frame. Similarly, if you meditatively concentrate on a yantra, you will create within your mind a negative impression of its particular figure or its digits. These can be seen within after some special meditation practices. If you then can make certain invocations when the yantra appears within you, your pilgrimage into the spiritual realm immediately begins.

There is a story in the life of Mulla Nasruddin . . .

Nasruddin lost his donkey – and his donkey was his only wealth. He searched for him through the whole village; all the villagers joined in the search, but without success. Then people said that as it was a holy month and many pilgrims were passing through the town, perhaps the donkey had followed them. Otherwise, since they had searched all over the town and had not been able to find him, Nasruddin should accept that the donkey was lost.

But Nasruddin said he would make one last attempt to find him. Right there he stood still and closed his eyes. Then he bent down and started walking on all fours. He walked around the house and then the garden, and finally he reached a large pit into which his donkey had fallen. His friends were surprised and asked him what his trick was.

Nasruddin said, 'I thought, if a man cannot find a donkey, then the key to finding it is not with him – to find the donkey I have to become like a donkey. So when I began to feel like a donkey, I thought if I was a donkey looking for a donkey where would I look? As soon as I thought that way, I went down on my hands and knees and started walking like a donkey. I do not know how I found the place, but when I opened my eyes I saw that I had reached the pit – and there was my donkey!'

Nasruddin is a Sufi saint. Anyone can read this story and laugh it off as a joke, but there is a key in it. It is a key to searching, and in a spiritual sense this is the only way to search. So every place of pilgrimage has keys and yantras. The main reason for the existence of such places is that they put you in the middle of a charged current – which you can flow with.

Another important fact is that everything in a man's life – except his consciousness – is made of matter, but we do not know what that inner consciousness is. We know only our body, and the body is in every way related to matter.

Let us now try to understand something about alchemy, so that you can understand the second meaning of a place of pilgrimage.

The alchemists' processes are processes of religion. Alchemists say that if water is converted into steam, and then that steam is converted back into water, and the water is again converted into steam – if you do this again and again, thousands of times – this water acquires a special quality not found in ordinary water. Earlier, this assertion was taken to be a joke: How could the quality of the water change? If you repeatedly distill water, what difference can it make? The water will remain distilled. But now, science has also accepted the fact that the quality of such water does change – although just how it happens is not known. There is no doubt there is a qualitative change in the water, and repeating the experiment hundreds of thousands of times produces an even better quality of water.

You may not be aware that seventy percent of your body is made up of water – the chemical composition is just like sea water. If you do not eat enough salt, the salt content within your body diminishes, becomes less than that of sea water. If the percentage of salt in your body is changed, there will be changes in your consciousness. If you drink water which has been distilled one hundred thousand times, it brings about changes in many of your desires and attitudes. The alchemists were doing experiments like this. Someone would boil and reboil water day in day out. Distilling water hundreds of thousands of times may take several years, but the alchemist did this; someone would boil and reboil water day in day out.

It brings about two types of changes: the first will be in that person's mind. Doing the same thing again and again can become boring after a few days. If out of boredom he stops the process, he will go back to his old state of mind, but that moment of boredom is the turning point. If he continues in spite of the boredom, he will give birth to a new consciousness.

If you go to sleep at ten o'clock every night, then at exactly that time you will feel sleepy. But if you decide not to sleep and stay awake, after half an hour you would expect to become sleepier – but what actually happens is that you feel fresher than in the morning. There was a turning point at ten o'clock: it was your habit to sleep then, but if you ignore your habit you break the body's automatic pattern. And when the body realizes that it will have to stay awake, it releases fresh energy from a reservoir which it keeps for emergencies, and you feel fresher than ever.

Now the person who has distilled water a thousand times becomes bored, but his master will tell him to continue – maybe for ten or fifteen years! A point will come when he feels that if he distills the water one more time, he will not be able to bear it, he will drop down dead. But his master will insist he continue the process, whatever the consequences, so on one hand the quality of the water will change, and on the other, his consciousness will also slowly become transformed – and then the use of this special water brings transformation in the user's consciousness.

It is like the water of the River Ganges. Up to now, scientists have not been able to understand why there are certain qualities in its waters which cannot be found in the water of any other river of the world. Even the rivers that flow from the same mountain from which the Ganges flows do not have the same qualities as the Ganges. The mountain is the same, the same clouds shower water over it, the ice from the same peak melts and flows into the waters of all the rivers, but the quality of their water differs. It is difficult to prove it – there are things which are difficult to prove – but the whole of the Ganges is an alchemical experiment. There are many things in what I am saying which will be difficult to prove, but the Ganges is no ordinary river. It has been attempted to treat the whole river alchemically – that is why Hindus have so many of their holy places of pilgrimage on the banks of the Ganges. It was a great experiment to give something special to the waters of the Ganges.

Now chemists and scientists have also agreed there is something special about its waters. If you save the water of any other river it will spoil and go bad, but the water of the Ganges does not, however long it is stored. You can keep this water for years without it changing, whereas if you keep water from any other river, you will find it becomes foul within a few weeks. The water of the Ganges keeps its purity and remains unchanged for years.

If you throw dead bodies into other rivers, the river becomes dirty and will begin to smell badly, but the Ganges absorbs thousands of dead bodies without stinking. And there is another amazing thing: although bones do not normally dissolve in water, they do in the water of the Ganges – nothing remains. In the Ganges everything soon disintegrates, returning to its original elements. Hence the insistence on dead bodies being thrown into the Ganges because in any other river, or through other methods of disposing of the dead, the bones take years to disintegrate, but the Ganges does the work quickly – it is alchemical, this is the purpose for which it was created.

The Ganges does not flow like any ordinary river from a mountain, it has been *made* to flow. This phenomenon is not easy to grasp. Gangotri, the place where the Ganges is said to have its source, is a very small point and it is not the real source of the Ganges. The real always needs to be protected, hidden. What is there is a facade. Pilgrims go there, make their salutations and then return home. The real Gangotri has always been hidden and protected for thousands of years. It is not possible to reach there by ordinary means, but only by astral travel. It is not possible to reach there with the physical body.

I told you earlier about Alkufa, the city of the Sufis – there you can reach physically, even unintentionally. Because if you go in search of it, you can be given the wrong map, but if you have not set out to search for it, you can just reach there without meaning to, by accident. So you can stumble across Alkufa, but the real Gangotri cannot be reached with the physical body, only with the astral body. The real Gangotri cannot be seen with the physical eyes. In meditation the physical body has to be left behind, and then the astral body can travel to Gangotri – then and then only will one understand the secret of the special qualities of the water of the Ganges. That is why I said it cannot be proved, there is no way to prove it. At the source, from where the Ganges flows, its waters have been treated alchemically; on both banks at the source of the river, Hindus have made places of pilgrimage.

You may wonder why all the Hindu places of pilgrimage are on the banks of rivers, while all the Jainas' are on mountain tops. Jainas make their places of pilgrimage only on mountains that are absolutely dry and without any greenery. Mountains with vegetation and trees will be rejected; even beautiful mountains like the Himalayas have been ignored. If just any mountain would do, there could be none better than those of the Himalayas, but the Jainas wanted a dry mountain, open to the scorching sun, with the least possible vegetation and no water. The reason is that the alchemical changes which they are experimenting on are connected to the fire element of the body; the Hindu alchemy on the other hand is related to the element of water.

Both have their separate keys. Hindus would never think of having a *tirtha* that was not within the vicinity of water, of a river flowing by, with the beauty of green vegetation. They experiment with the element of water, and all their places of pilgrimage depend on water, and are created through water; whereas Jainas are working on the element of fire, and so they depend more on the generation of heat in the body.

Hindu scriptures and monks emphasize the water element, so a Hindu sannyasin consumes enough milk, curd, and clarified butter, to maintain sufficient humidity or moisture within his body. Without sufficient moisture, the Hindu key will not function. On the other hand the whole effort of the Jainas is to produce a dryness within, so Jaina monks don't even take a bath because they want to preserve a state of dryness. These Jaina sadhus become dirty and they stink! But they are not able to explain *why* they do not take baths. Why do they only very sparingly wash themselves? Water is not their key, but fire, and the fire element is their austerity and self-mortification. Their intention is to arouse fire internally in every possible way. If they pour water on their bodies, the fire within will be weakened. So you will find the Jaina monk on barren, dry mountains, without greenery and water, where everything is hot and he is surrounded only by stones.

All religions use fasting, but except for Jainism not many religions prohibit water during fasting. Jainas who are householders are advised that even if they cannot do without water at other times, at least they should avoid drinking water at night. But all they understand this to mean is that they should not drink at night because they might unknowingly kill unseen germs and insects. In fact, all these rules are meant to intensify the fire element. Another interesting fact is that if a man drinks a minimum amount of water, as Mahavira used to, it helps to preserve his celibacy because the semen will begin to dry up. Even a little moisture can make the semen flow.

All authentic Jaina places of pilgrimage will be in the mountains; they are always created remote from any sources of water. Later, in imitation, Jainas also created some places of pilgrimage near water, but these are completely meaningless – they are not authentic. The authentic Hindu *tirtha* will be on the banks of a river, in a beautiful, lush-green place, but the mountains chosen by Jainas are ugly because the beauty of a mountain is lost when there is no greenery.

Jaina monks will not take a bath or clean their teeth: why use even the amount of water needed for brushing your teeth? The whole principle of dryness has to be understood properly to understand the Jaina scriptures. All of their austerities are to arouse the internal fire, and if the connection with water is completely broken, this is a negative way to fan the fire.

Inside us there is a balance of all the elements: if you want to go on a spiritual journey through one of the elements, the balance will have to be broken by dropping the use of the opposite element which balances it. So if you concentrate on the fire element, water will become inimical to your work because the less water in the body, the better the fire will burn within.

The Ganges is a deep chemical and alchemical experiment – after taking a bath in the Ganges, an individual will enter the *tirtha*. As soon as he takes a bath, the water element within his body is transformed. This transformation will only last a short time, but if the experiments are done rightly the spiritual journey begins. Remember, if someone who has begun living on the water of the Ganges takes any other water, it will not suit him and will create difficulties.

Attempts have been made to create the qualities of the Ganges in many other places, in other rivers, but they have failed because the real keys for doing so have been lost. Bathing in the Ganges and then immediately entering prayer or worship, going into a temple or to a holy place, is only a way of using the outer for the inner spiritual journey. And many other elements were also made use of in the places of pilgrimage. They were created with meticulous care.

For instance, the Egyptian pyramids are *tirthas* of an old, lost civilization. One interesting fact about the pyramids is that there is complete darkness inside. Scientists think it is unlikely electricity existed when the pyramids were built – some were constructed ten thousand years ago, others twenty thousand years ago. It is possible people entered them with the help of burning torches, but there are no signs of smoke anywhere on the walls or ceilings of the pyramids. The paths within the pyramids are very long, with many twists and turns, and along them it is very dark. There could not have been electricity because there are no signs of electric fittings or a source of power supply. Torches burning oil or ghee would have left some signs of smoke. So the problem arises as to how people moved inside. And if no one went in, as some people suggest, why were so many paths made? There are many paths, staircases, doors and internal windows, and also places for people to sit or stand about, but what was all this for? It has remained an unsolved puzzle. And it will never become clear as long as the notion persists that the pyramids were built at some emperor's whim.

They were actually *tirthas*. When someone experiments with the inner fire in the right way, his body emanates a light. Such people became qualified to enter the pyramids. Neither electricity nor torches were ever needed: their body light was sufficient to be able to move around inside the pyramid. But this body light is only produced through special meditative practices with the fire element. So producing the body light was itself the test of people's right to enter.

In the early nineteen hundreds, when investigations were being done on the pyramids, one of the scientists' assistants became lost. With the help of searchlights they looked everywhere for him, but for twenty-four hours he could not be found. Then, after twenty-four hours, sometime around two o'clock in the morning, he came running toward them, almost deranged.

He said, 'I was feeling my way in the darkness and I suddenly became aware of an opening. I went through it, and as soon as I did the door shut behind me. When I looked back the door was already closed. Yet when I had first approached it, there was only an open passage, nothing there like a door, but as soon as I entered that part of the passage, a door closed behind me; a heavy rock slid down, sealing off the exit. I shouted, but there was no response. I had no choice but to keep walking, and the things I saw... It's difficult to describe!'

It is true he was lost for twenty-four hours and when he was found he was half insane, but what he described he had seen was incredible. The whole search party then tried to find the door, but was not able to. He could neither show where he had entered nor where he had come out, so it was concluded the man must have either fainted, or gone to sleep and dreamed – but anyway, whatever he related was recorded.

Sometime after, during further explorations, the group found a manuscript which described things similar to what the man had related. So the mystery deepened. It was thought these things were in some sealed-off room which only opened up under the influence of someone in a certain psychic state. It had perhaps been accidental, or perhaps just a coincidence: triggered by his mental state the man may have unknowingly become attuned to the state in which the opening happens. It must have been like this because although the man was not able to prove his experience, the door had nevertheless opened.

So the secret places about which I am talking have their doors, and there are ways through which one can enter into them, but these are special esoteric keys. In these *tirthas* there are arrangements under whose influence one's consciousness is triggered: for example, all the rooms and halls of the pyramids, their dimensions, their size.

You may have experienced sometimes where a roof is set rather low: even though it does not touch you, you feel something within you is compressed, contracted. Nothing actually compresses you, but within you something feels compressed. When you enter a place where the ceiling is very high, you have a feeling of something expanding within. A room can be built in such a way that its dimensions encourage meditation.

The exact measurements of a room in which meditation is easiest were discovered through experimentation. Certain measurements of a room can be used to help you either expand or contract your consciousness. The color scheme outside and inside rooms, the fragrance in the room, and also the acoustics, can be devised in such a way as to help meditation.

All *tirthas* had their own music. In fact, all music was born in such places, and the music was originally created by meditators. Not only the art of music, but all dance originated in temples. Fragrance was also first used in temples. When it was realized one could reach the divine with the help of music, it was also realized one could go in the opposite direction through music.

If a certain fragrance can help one go toward the divine, then with another fragrance one can also go toward sensuality. If one can go into meditation more quickly and easily in a certain kind of room, there are other kinds which can prevent meditation.

In China there are specially constructed rooms in which prisoners can be brainwashed; the dimensions are predetermined, and any changes to those dimensions make brainwashing difficult. After many experiments the exact height, width, and breadth of such rooms were determined so that as soon as a prisoner is brought into the room, his mind begins to become affected. It was also determined exactly how long it will take before his mind becomes deranged and begins to deteriorate. A certain sound was created to speed up the process of deterioration, and if a particular place on his head is hit, the deterioration will be even faster.

A water pot is suspended above the prisoner's head and water slowly drips onto him in a particular rhythm. Drop by drop, the water falls on that spot on his head for twenty-four hours. The prisoner is not allowed to move from that position; he cannot sit, he has to stand. Within half an hour he becomes so bored that the sound seems to become louder and louder, shattering – so much so that he begins to feel as if a mountain is falling on top of him. This repetitive sound in the enclosure for twenty-four hours – in that particularly designed room – will shatter a person's mind; when he comes out he will not be the same person. The technique will have broken him down in every way.

All methods to help the seeker were discovered in *tirthas* and temples. The bells hanging in the temple, the sounds that emanate, the incense, the flowers, their fragrance, were all specially arranged. It was all designed to maintain a certain harmony whose continuity would not be broken, day or night.

If *arti*, a ritual using a lighted lamp, is to be done, it is always performed at a fixed time in the morning, for a fixed length of time, using a fixed mantra; at a fixed time in the middle of the day, for a fixed length of time, using a fixed mantra; and at a fixed time in the evening, for a fixed length of time, with a fixed mantra. The sound waves will go on vibrating in the room – a new one taking over before the old one has completely died. The ritual goes on at regular intervals, year after year, for thousands of years.

Just as I told you earlier that when water is repeatedly distilled, it changes its quality, if a sound is created within a room thousands of times, the vibrations of that room and the quality of that room change. If a seeker is taken into that room, his transformation will be helped. Since our whole individuality is built from matter, whatever changes are brought about in matter will affect our individuality too. Man is such an extrovert that it is easier to change him from the outside – inner changes are difficult in the beginning – so a system was devised through which matter could be arranged to help one transform on a physical level.

There is one other thing to be understood. Ordinarily we have the illusion that we are all separate individuals. This is a wrong belief. There are many of us sitting here, but if all of us sit silently, there will no longer be separate individuals, only one individuality – one individuality of silence will remain, and our consciousnesses will begin to vibrate together and flow into each other.

The *tirtha* is a mass experiment. On a special day in the year, hundreds of thousands of people gather at a *tirtha*, all with one longing, one aspiration. People will come from hundreds of miles away to be together at a certain hour, under a certain star or constellation. With so many people and this one longing, this one aspiration, one prayer and one aim, a pool of consciousness is created. Then there are no longer many individuals.

If we look at the huge gatherings at the Kumbha Mela festival, we do not see one individual, we see just a crowd without a face. In this huge crowd, separate faces cannot be found, just a faceless crowd of millions of people. When ten million people have gathered, there is no longer any point in trying to know who is who. Who is poor and who is rich? Who is a king and who is a beggar? There is no meaning in trying to make a distinction. Everyone has become faceless. The consciousnesses of everyone have begun to flow into each other. If the consciousnesses of these ten million people can be pooled, if they can become one integrated consciousness, then it is easier for the divine to enter this collective consciousness than to enter so many individuals separately. It is a bigger field of contact.

Nietzsche has written somewhere that he was walking in a garden when his foot touched a centipede, which immediately rolled up and withdrew. Nietzsche was very puzzled as to why it behaved like this. He wrote that after thinking about it for some time, he realized the insect was trying to decrease its field of contact, in order to prevent being hurt. With a larger insect there are more chances it will be trodden on and killed because it takes up a bigger area. So this is how a small insect protects itself, by reducing its field of contact. And the faster an insect is able to roll up and withdraw, the more chance it has of protecting itself.

So when human consciousness forms a bigger contact field, the possibility of the divine descending into it becomes greater. The descending of the divine is a great happening. The greater the happening, the greater the place we have to create for it.

The original form of prayer was group oriented; individual prayer was born much later when the individual became more egoistic, and it was more difficult for him to melt with others. So, from the time individual prayer began in the world, the real benefits of prayer were lost. In fact, prayer cannot be individual. When we are invoking such a great force as the divine, the larger a contact field we provide, the easier it is for that force to descend.

In this sense, *tirthas* create large contact fields. Again, when such a field is created at a particular moment, on a particular day, under a certain constellation, and in a particular place, the chances are better. These were sure methods. At the same hour, under the same constellation formations, the contact has taken place on earlier occasions also. And the whole life-system is cyclical. These were sure methods.

It should be understood that the life system is periodical: the monsoon begins at a particular time of the year. If it does not happen this way today, it is because of our interference; it used to be fairly fixed, even to the day and the hour. Summer, winter, and spring all used to arrive at particular times. Even our bodies work that way: women's menstruation is regulated, and related in some way to the cycles of the moon. If the body is healthy and normal, menstruation occurs after twenty-eight days. If the cycle is broken, then somewhere within the body of that woman something has gone wrong.

All events repeat in a cyclical order. If the coming of the divine has happened at a particular moment – on a certain day, in a certain month – next year at the same time you can expect it to happen again. The chances are enhanced. This moment has become empowered, and at this moment the divine energy can flow again. So year after year, for hundreds of years, people have gathered together to wait at certain *tirthas*. If it has happened many, many times, then it becomes more likely that at this particular moment the event will repeat; in fact, it almost becomes a certainty.

For example, at the time of the Kumbha Mela festival there are many disputes and quarrels over who will take the first dip in the Ganges because it is impossible for hundreds of thousands of people to simultaneously take a dip. The special moment is well defined, subtle, and of short duration. So, who will take the first dip at the right moment? It belongs to those people whose traditions have searched for and discovered the moment initially; they will be the first.

Sometimes the right moment is missed by just a fraction. The moment when the divine descends is just like a flash of lightning. It simply flashes and is gone. If you are completely open and totally aware at that moment, then there will be the experience of the happening; if at that moment you are sleepy and unaware, the event will be lost to you.

The third use of the *tirtha* was a group experience, in which the divine could be invited to descend on a vast scale. At a time when people were innocent and simple this used to happen very easily, it was not like today. *Tirthas* had more relevance in those days: no one returned from them empty-handed, but the pilgrim of today does return empty-handed – and so he has to go again and again. In those days people were returning transformed without fail, but these happenings belong to very innocent and simple societies. The more innocent and simple a society is, the less people are aware of their individual personalities, and the more successful such a group experience can be.

Even today, there are primitive tribal communities in which the individual is unaware of his personality. There is less of an idea of 'I,' and more of 'we.' There are a few tribal languages in which the word 'I' does not exist. Tribals speak in the language of 'we.' It is not because of the language that the concept of 'I' does not exist, but because their life is so community oriented. This has sometimes produced some really surprising results.

Some Westerners invaded a small island near Singapore one time. The chief of the tribe came to the shore and told the invaders that his people were unarmed, but were not going to be slaves. The Westerners then proceeded to enslave them. The tribe refused to fight, saying they knew how to die. The

Westerners could not believe this, they thought no one would die just like that – but one of the most historic events took place right there. Five hundred tribesmen gathered together on the seashore. The Westerners could not believe their eyes: first, the chief fell down and died; then, one after the other, all the others fell to the ground and died – without being hit by a weapon. The Westerners were overwhelmed, and after seeing this they left.

At first the Westerners had thought they were just falling down out of fear, but when they approached them they found all the tribesmen had actually died. To this day, nobody really knows what happened there.

If the consciousness of 'we' is predominant, death can be contagious. If one dies, then death spreads. Some animals die like that. If one sheep dies, then death spreads. Sheep do not have any awareness of 'I,' only of 'we'. If you see sheep walking, it is as if they are all joined together, as if only one life is moving. If one sheep dies, the others feel like dying; an inner feeling to die begins to spread.

So when the society was more conscious of the feeling of 'we' and there was not much awareness of 'I,' the *tirthas* were very effective. The utility of such places has been lost in the same proportion as the awareness of 'I' increased.

The final thing to be understood about the *tirtha* is the value of symbolic acts. For example, someone comes to Jesus and confesses his sins. Jesus puts his hand on that person's head and says, 'Go, all your sins are forgiven.' Now how can Jesus forgive them, just by putting his hand on someone's head? And who is Jesus to forgive anyone's sins? If a person has committed a murder, how can he be forgiven like this? In India it is said, no matter what sins may have been committed, if you take a bath in the Ganges you will be free from your sins. It seems insane. How can someone who has committed theft, who has defrauded people, who has killed someone, become freed of his sins by bathing in the Ganges?

Here two things need to be understood. The real issue is not the sin, but the memory of it. It is not the sin – the act of sinning – that clings to you, but the memory of it. If you have killed someone, the memory of it will haunt you like a nightmare your whole life. Those who know of inner things say that whether a murder is committed or not, it is just part of a drama, and is not very important. No one dies nor can anyone be killed, but the memory of the murder weighs heavily on your chest like a stone. The act was committed and disappeared into the infinite; it was absorbed by the infinite. The reality is that *all* acts belong to the infinite; you are unnecessarily becoming disturbed. If you committed a theft, it was done through you by the infinite. If you killed someone, it was done through you by the infinite. You are unnecessarily getting in the way because of your memory of the act, and that memory is a burden on you.

Jesus says, 'Repent, and I will take away your sins' – and someone who trusts in Jesus returns home unburdened and purified. In reality Jesus does not free you from your sins, but from the *memory* of your sins. The memory is the real thing – Jesus only removes that. Similarly, the Ganges does not free you from your sins, but can free you from the memory of them. If someone trusts in the Ganges, and believes that if he bathes in it he will be free of all sins, if the collective unconscious, built up over thousands of years, reinforces this belief, and if the society in which he is living also confirms this strong belief – then he will be freed. Bathing cannot make a person free from the sin as such because the sin has already been committed – nothing can be done about the theft that has been committed, or the murder that has been committed; nothing can be done about that – but when a person with such a belief emerges from the

Ganges, his trust in its purity and power frees him from the feeling of guilt, even though the bathing is only a symbolic act.

How long can Jesus live on earth? How many sinners can he meet? How many of them can repent? Time is very short, and what will happen when Jesus is not there? Hindus have found a more permanent arrangement, connecting confession with a river, not a person. The river goes on receiving confessions and forgiving people. The river is infinite, its flow is steady and permanent – how long can Jesus live? He was able to work for barely three years, from the age of thirty to thirty-three. How many sinners could confess within the span of three years? How many sinners could reach him? On how many could he put his hand? So Hindu seers entrust this phenomenon to an impersonal river, not to a person.

If someone goes to a *tirtha* he will return free and unburdened, he will be free of the memory of his sin – it is the memory that has become a bondage. The culprit is the shadow of the sin that follows you. It is possible to be free from it, but there is one condition: the most important condition is that you have total faith – faith in the idea you will become free of the sin. And how can such a faith happen in you? – it can happen if you know this has been happening for thousands of years. It cannot be otherwise; this is how it has been for thousands of years.

There are a few *tirthas* that are eternal – Kashi is one of them. There has never been a time on earth when Kashi, Varanasi, was not a *tirtha*. It is man's oldest place of pilgrimage, hence it is of great value as a long stream of consciousness. So many people have been liberated, experienced peace and sacredness there, the sins of so many have been washed away there – a long, long continuity, and so the suggestion that one can be freed of sin has gone deeper and deeper. This suggestion becomes faith to a simple mind, and if such trust is there, the holy place becomes effective; otherwise it is useless. Without your cooperation, a *tirtha* cannot help you. And you will be able to give your cooperation only if the holy place has continuity, history.

Hindus say that Kashi – the city of Shiva – is not a part of this earth, but a place apart; it is separate and indestructible. Many towns will be built and destroyed, but Kashi will remain forever – which is amazing because human beings come and go. Buddha went to Kashi, Jaina tirthankaras were born in Kashi, Shankaracharya also went to Kashi, Kabir lived in Kashi. Kashi has seen tirthankaras, avatars and saints, but all are no more; except for Kashi, not one of them remains. The sacredness of all these people, their spiritual merit, their life currents, their collective fragrance, has been absorbed by Kashi and still exists. This makes Kashi separate from the earth, at least metaphysically. It stands out; it has acquired an eternal form of its own; it has acquired a personality of its own.

Buddha has walked on this city's roads, and Kabir has given religious discourses in its lanes. Now it has all become a story, a dream, but Kashi has assimilated all this within itself and it goes on living. If someone with absolute trust and faith enters this city, he will again see Buddha walking on its roads, he will again see Parshvanath walking on its roads, he will see Tulsidas and Kabir. If you approach Kashi sympathetically, then it is not just an ordinary city like Mumbai or London; it will take on a unique spiritual form. Its consciousness is ancient and eternal. History may be lost, civilizations may be born and destroyed, may come and go, but Kashi's inner life flow is continuous. Walking on its roads, bathing near the banks of its river, the Ganges, and sitting in meditation in Kashi, you also become a part of its inner flow. To think 'I alone can do everything' is dangerous. Divine help is available in many forms. Its help can be sought through its temples and holy places. They are designed to provide just that help.

I have told you some things which can be easily understood and perceived by your intellect in order to explain the *tirtha* to you, but that is not enough. There are many things connected with such places which cannot be understood – but they do happen. Such things cannot be intellectually clarified or made into mathematical formulas – but they do happen.

I will tell you about two or three things that happen. If you sit somewhere alone in meditation, you are unlikely to feel the presence of any souls who may be around you, but in a *tirtha* the experience of such presence can be very powerful. It may become so deep sometimes that you feel your own presence less than that of the others.

For example, Kailash has been a holy place for Hindus as well as for Tibetan Buddhists. Kailash is absolutely desolate: it has no houses and no human population – no worshippers, no priests – but whoever sits in meditation at Kailash will find it fully inhabited. From the moment you reach Kailash, if you are capable of going into meditation you will say it is inhabited by many souls, and wonderful ones too, but if you go there and cannot meditate, then Kailash will be empty for you.

Researchers believe there are no inhabitants on the moon, but those who have some experience of Kailash will not agree. Astronauts will not find any signs of habitation there, but it does not necessarily follow that there is no one there just because the astronauts don't find anyone.

In Jaina scriptures there are detailed descriptions of the gods residing on the moon, but since astronauts have reported there is no life on the moon the Jaina saints and monks have been embarrassed. All they can say in their own ignorance is the astronauts have not reached the *real* moon, otherwise they would have to admit their scriptures are wrong.

Recently, someone in Gujarat was telling me that a Jaina monk was collecting funds to prove the astronauts have not reached the real moon. This is not something which can be proved – the astronauts *did* reach the real moon – but the difficulty is that Jaina scriptures say certain gods live there. It is written in their books – they themselves do not know – so with their ordinary intelligence, Jaina monks will say the astronauts did not reach the real moon because to them the scriptures cannot be wrong. Some other Jaina monk claimed the astronauts actually arrived on some huge satellites which are situated near the moon, not on the moon itself. All this is ridiculous, madness, but there are reasons behind this madness. There has been a Jaina belief, over twenty thousand years old, that there is life on the moon, but they do not know what kind of life – this life form is like that of Kailash or any other *tirtha*.

When you get off the train at Kashi station, you see the gross form of Kashi, made of mud and stone. Any tourist can go there and return home, but there is a spiritual form of Kashi which only those who can move inward will be able to reach – those who can go deep into meditation – for them Kashi will be different, very beautiful, beyond imagination. Whereas the earthly Kashi is dirtier and more foul-smelling than any other city – that is only the visible Kashi.

Some would say that the other Kashi, the beautiful one, exists only in the imagination of the poet – but this Kashi is also really there. The earthly Kashi is only a contact field for the invisible Kashi. Someone who arrives by train will return home having only visited the gross Kashi, but someone who comes seated in the vehicle of meditation will be able to contact the spiritual Kashi. Someone who reaches through meditation reaches the spiritual Kashi: on the remote banks of this very Kashi, this gross Kashi, he might come across people he could never have imagined meeting.

Just now I said that on the mountain called Kailash there is an unearthly form of life. It is more or less certain about five hundred Buddhist *siddhas* are always there; five hundred individuals who are enlightened buddhas will always remain on Kailash. If one of them has to move on some other journey, he will not go until another buddha arrives to take his place – a minimum of five hundred enlightened buddhas must always stay there to make Kailash a *tirtha*.

But it is not something easily grasped by the intellect – hence I never talked about it. Kashi has a fixed number of enlightened ones who always stay there. Any one of them can only move on when there is a replacement. They are the real *tirtha*, and only when one meets them has one really entered the *tirtha*.

But it is only possible to meet them when there is a fixed physical location – otherwise where would you search for and meet disembodied souls? So Kashi is a place where you can sit in meditation and enter the inner world where it is possible to communicate with such souls.

A *tirtha* cannot be understood intellectually because it has nothing to do with the intellect. The real *tirtha* is hidden somewhere near the physical signs of it.

Another important thing is that when an enlightened person gives up the physical body, his compassion compels him to leave some physical signs behind to help those who walked with him, who did everything suggested and made a lot of effort to become enlightened, but did not yet succeed. Some guiding indications and symbols should be left for them so that if they need to they can establish a connection with him. In this world, although physical bodies are lost, no soul ever is, so some keys have to be left behind in order to make contact with these disembodied souls.

In relation to these keys, *tirthas* do the same work as is done by radar today: radar reaches where the eyes cannot. Stars that cannot be seen with the eyes can be detected by radar. *Tirthas* are spiritual radars; through the *tirtha*, communication can be established between those who are no longer in their bodies and those who are here. *Tirthas* were established by those who left, for those who are still on the path, who have not yet reached, for those who could still go astray. Those left behind may occasionally need to ask something, to know something which may be absolutely necessary for further progress, and without which they may go astray. They do not know what their future is, they do not know the road ahead; and so for such seekers in need, special arrangements were created – such as *tirthas*, temples, mantras, statues, and so on. They are all rituals, but still they are definite processes to be gone through.

If a primitive aboriginal were brought into your house, and saw that whenever you want light you get up from your chair, walk ten feet to the nearest wall, flip a switch and there is light – he would never be able to figure out there is a wire behind the wall connecting the switch with the bulb; there is no way for him to figure it out. He might even think there is some magic, and that your getting up and going to the wall to flick a certain switch is a kind of ritual. The flicking of the first switch turns on the light, the second turns on the fan, and the third one the radio – it is not just at random. He does not know about electricity and he would think you were performing some magic near the wall, some ritual.

But suppose that one day when you were not home, and the electricity went off, this primitive person went to the wall and performed the ritual of flipping on the switch. When he found there was no light, and that neither the fan nor the radio would come on, he would think he had made some mistake in the ritual – that he had not taken the right number of steps from the chair to the wall, or that he had not put the right foot down first or you had been humming a mantra while flipping the switch on. He would not be able to understand, or have any idea about the electrical network.

In relation to religion similar things happen: what we call religious rituals are the outward, superficial motions that we observe. Those who know nothing of the esoteric structure also go through the same motions. Sometimes, when something happens, we feel that perhaps the rituals are helpful. At other times, when nothing happens, we feel that earlier successes must have been accidental because if the ritual was right, it should always produce a result. So whatever we do not understand appears to be just a ritual laid on from the outside. This even happens to those people who are highly intellectual – because in a way intellect is childish, and in a sense an intellectual person is juvenile. Intellect cannot take you very deep.

A hundred years ago, when the gramophone was introduced into France, when a scientist announced he had invented the gramophone, the French academy of sciences convened to verify his claim. The scientist began the demonstration by putting on a record. The president of the academy watched carefully for a while, and then suddenly got up and took hold of the inventor by the neck! He thought the scientist was playing a trick with his throat: How could a voice come out of this machine? He squeezed his neck even tighter – but the voice continued! The inventor had never expected this from a scientist; he became frightened and asked the president what he was doing. He said it was no trick and asked the president to leave the room with him – the voice of the gramophone could still be heard. All the other scientists present protested as well and said it must be some trick, the work of the Devil – otherwise how could a small disc start speaking? Today we can laugh at this because we know what a gramophone is. If we did not, we would have reacted in a similar way.

If one day an atomic war destroys the whole of civilization except for a record player that happens to be with an aboriginal tribesman, and if he puts that record player on, the remaining population of the tribe may kill him because he will not be able to explain how the record speaks. Even you may not be able to explain how a record 'speaks.'

It is interesting to note that all civilizations live through beliefs, faith. Only three or four people have the keys; the rest just have faith. You flick on a switch and there is light; you do it daily, but can you explain how it happens? Just a few people hold the keys to a civilization – the remaining people are only living somehow – but when these keys become lost, those people who have just been living somehow will lose confidence: they will be in difficulty if one day the light bulb does not light up.

The *tirtha* and the temple have their own science, and this science contains specific rules for the whole process. The second step follows the first, and the third follows the second; if even one step is missed, the intended result will not follow.

It should also be understood that once a civilization is highly developed, once any science becomes well developed, its practices become simplified – they do not remain complex. But as long as technology is not well developed, the processes remain very complicated. For example, what could be easier than flicking a switch to produce light? But do you think it was like this for the inventors of these electrical devices? What could be easier and simpler than my voice being recorded while I speak? It does not take much, but do you think it was as simple to invent the tape recorder? If someone were to ask me how many words are recorded on this tape recorder, I would say one has only to speak and one's voice is recorded – but it took a long time to develop the tape recorder. Now the process is simplified, and because it has been simplified, this technology could reach to the common man – the common man only has the end results in his hands.

Religion too is like this. When a Mahavira is working on some religious principles, he stakes his life on them, but you come to know the evolved process very easily – it becomes as easy for you as pressing a button. But this is the real difficulty: the inventor gets lost, and only the button remains in your hand – and you may not be able to explain how to activate the process, or how it will work.

At the moment, scientists in America and Russia are very keen to evolve telepathic methods to communicate with their astronauts in space. The spaceship Luna was lost in space because its radio stopped working, so they are alert to the danger of relying too much on technology in space. If radio contact is lost, the astronauts are lost forever; we may not be able to re-establish contact with them. While in space, they may discover something which they may want to report back to earth, but they may not be able to contact us. Some alternative method is needed, so even if the equipment does not work, thoughts can still be transmitted – so American and Russian scientists are very keen on developing telepathy.

America appointed a commission to collect knowledge existing anywhere in the world related to telepathy. After some three or four years, the commission reported that telepathic communication is possible, but the people who are able to use it are not able to explain how it is done.

In the report there is an account of a certain tribe in the Amazon. In every village of this tribe there is a particular kind of small tree, and through the help of this tree the tribe communicates messages from one village to the other. For example, if a man has gone to a nearby village to get some household requirements, and his wife suddenly remembers she has forgotten to ask him to bring a particular article, she goes to the tree and says to her husband, 'Hey look! Don't forget to bring such and such a thing' – and he gets the message. And in the evening when the husband arrives home, he has brought the article. The members of the commission watched this happening, and were very puzzled.

When we talk with someone on the telephone, a primitive person is bound to be puzzled. We are not because we know the system. And when we listen to the radio, there is nothing alarming about it for us because we know what it is. But we are certainly surprised when we are told there are people who transmit messages through a tree.

The members of the commission stayed with this tribe for three or four days and set up their own experiments. They talked to the people of the village, but no one was able to explain how the transmission of messages happened – they could only say it had always happened. They took care the tree did not die, and a ritual was made of taking cuttings of its branches. Their fathers and their forefathers had always used the tree to pass on messages, but they did not know how it worked because what they actually had in their hands was a simplified process. The vital energy of the tree was being used for telepathy, but how it all began, how the tree cooperated with it and started functioning like this for thousands of years, the tribal people did not know. The key has been lost with the people who discovered it, but they go on replanting the tree and using it for this purpose.

Buddhists do not allow the original bodhi tree – the one under which Buddha became enlightened – to die. Now you can understand why. When the original tree was withering, King Ashoka sent one of its branches to Sri Lanka – that branch grew into a tree and is still there. A branch of it was brought back to India and planted in Bodhgaya. The same tree has been kept in continuity. The Bodhgaya *tirtha* is valuable because of that tree.

When Buddha became enlightened the tree must have deeply absorbed something of Buddha's consciousness. The experience of enlightenment happening to Buddha was an unprecedented and extraordinary event. If lightning strikes a tree, the tree will be burned, so it is not difficult to imagine that when the lightning of consciousness struck Buddha, the tree too became enlightened in some way.

Buddha must have given some secret instructions not to allow the tree to die. He said, 'Don't worship me – it is enough to worship this tree.' That is why for five hundred years after his enlightenment there were no statues made of him – the bodhi tree was the idol and it was worshipped. In the pictures of the Buddhist temples of those days there is only the bodhi tree and the circular aura of Buddha, but no image of Buddha himself. That tree had its own experience of the event of enlightenment and became charged. Those who know use the tree to establish communication with Buddha.

So it is not the town of Bodhgaya, but the bodhi tree that is of value. Buddha walked and lived under that tree for a long time before his enlightenment; his footprints have been preserved under it. When Buddha became tired in meditation, he would walk around that tree for hours on end – he did not live with anyone as much as he did with that tree. He could not have lived with any human being with as much ease and innocence as he did with that tree. He slept under it, sat under it, and walked around it; he must have talked to it. The whole life energy of that tree was filled with, saturated with, and charged with Buddha.

When King Ashoka sent his son Mahendra to Sri Lanka, Mahendra asked, 'What shall I take with me as a gift?' Ashoka replied they had only one gift, and there could be no better gift in the world than the bodhi tree, and that he could take a branch of it as a gift. So the branch was taken to Sri Lanka. No other king on the earth has ever given a branch of a tree as a gift – can such a thing be a gift? But the whole of Sri Lanka was affected with the energy vibrating from the branch of that bodhi tree.

People say that Mahendra converted Sri Lanka to Buddhism, but they are wrong. The conversion of Sri Lanka happened through the branch of the bodhi tree: this branch turned the people toward Buddhism. Buddha had given a secret message that the branch should be sent to Sri Lanka, and the right time and the right person to carry it should be waited for. When the right person appeared, the branch was sent.

Mahendra and Sanghamitra were Buddhist monks who were alive during Buddha's time. The bodhi tree could not be sent to Sri Lanka through just anyone; only a person who had lived with Buddha, who had known Buddha, and who would not carry the branch simply as the branch of a tree, but as a living Buddha, could be entrusted with the task. One day, through some other person, it would have to be brought back to India from this very tree.

Someday, it will be worthwhile to talk about esoteric history which runs as an undercurrent to mundane history. The deeper history is where the actual roots are, where the original source is; otherwise there is a network of events that happen on the surface, that are printed in newspapers and books – but that is not the real history.

When we become capable of focusing our sight on the real history, it will become easier to understand the secrets of all these things.

3
The Occult Science of the Third Eye

BEFORE I TALK TO YOU ABOUT THE WEARING of the vermilion or sandal-paste mark on the forehead, I would like to tell you about two events. It will make things easier for you to understand. Both of them are historical facts.

In 1888, a person named Ramanuja was born into a poor brahmin family in South India. He became a very famous mathematician. He could not study much, but still his genius in mathematics was unique. Many well-educated mathematicians had earned a name as a result of being trained and guided by others for years, but Ramanuja was not even a matriculate and had had no training or guidance from anyone. Hence, those who know mathematics say there has never been a greater mathematical genius than Ramanuja.

With great difficulty he got a clerical job, but soon the news spread that he had an amazing talent for mathematics. Someone suggested he write a letter to the famous mathematician, Professor Hardy of Cambridge University, who was the most eminent mathematician of those days. Ramanuja did not write a letter, but rather solved two theorems of geometry and sent them to Hardy. Hardy was astonished to receive them, and could not believe someone so young could solve such theorems. He immediately wrote back to Ramanuja and invited him to England. When Hardy met him for the first time, he felt himself like a child before Ramanuja in the field of mathematics. The genius and capabilities of Ramanuja were such they could not have been due to mental powers: the intellect moves very slowly, thinking takes time, but Ramanuja did not take any time in responding to Hardy's questions. No sooner was the problem written down on the blackboard or put to him verbally than Ramanuja began to reply, without any gap for thinking. It was very difficult for the great mathematicians of the time to understand how it was happening. A problem which would take an eminent mathematician about six hours to solve – and then too he was not sure about his accuracy – Ramanuja would solve instantaneously, and unerringly.

It proved that Ramanuja was not replying through the medium of the mind. He was not very learned – he had actually failed in matriculation – and there were no other indications of intellectual ability, but in mathematics he was superhuman. Something was happening that was beyond the human mind.

Ramanuja died of tuberculosis when he was thirty-six. When he was in hospital, Hardy, along with two or three other mathematician friends, went to see him. As it happened, he parked his car in a place where Ramanuja could see its number plate. When Hardy entered Ramanuja's room, he told Hardy his number plate was unique: it had four special aspects to it. After that, Ramanuja died. It took Hardy six months to understand what Ramanuja meant, but he could only discover three of the four aspects. On his death he left a will that the research work on this number should continue, in order to discover the fourth aspect. Ramanuja had said there was a fourth, so there had to be. Twenty-two years after Hardy's death, the fourth aspect was discovered. Ramanuja had been right.

Whenever he began to look into a mathematical problem, something would happen in the space between his eyebrows. His eyeballs would turn upward, centering on that spot. In Yoga, that space is described as the third-eye point. It is called the third eye because if this eye becomes activated, it is possible to see events and scenes from different realms in their entirety. It is like looking out of your house through a small hole in the door, and suddenly, when the door opens, you see the whole sky. There is a space between the eyebrows where there is a small aperture which sometimes opens – as in the case of Ramanuja. His eyes rose to his third eye while solving a problem. Neither Hardy could understand this phenomenon nor would other Western mathematicians understand it in the near future.

I will tell you about another event in connection with the wearing of the vermilion mark, so you will be able to understand its relationship to the third eye.

Edgar Cayce died in 1945. Forty years before that, he fell sick, became unconscious and remained in a coma for three days. The doctors had lost all hope and said they could not find any way to bring him back to consciousness. They thought his unconsciousness had become so deep that perhaps he would never come out of it. Every kind of medicine was tried, but there were no signs of his regaining consciousness.

On the evening of the third day, the doctors announced they could do nothing more and that he would die within four to six hours, or if he lived, he would have brain damage – which would be worse than death – because as time passed the delicate veins and cells of his brain were disintegrating. But suddenly Cayce started to speak, even though he was in a coma. The doctors could not believe it: Cayce's body was unconscious, but he was speaking! He said he had fallen from a tree, his backbone was injured, and that was why he was unconscious. He also said that if he was not treated within six hours, his brain would be affected, and he would die. He suggested some herbal medicine which he should be given to drink, and said he should then recover within twelve hours.

The names of the herbs which he requested were not likely to have been known to Edgar Cayce, and at first the doctors thought what he was saying was just part of his brain damage because the substances he had suggested were not known to cure a condition such as his. But because Cayce had specifically mentioned them they thought they should try them. These substances were acquired, and given to Cayce – he fully recovered within twelve hours.

When later the incident was related to him, Cayce could not remember suggesting any such medication; he neither knew the names of the medication nor recognized them. But this event in Edgar Cayce's life was the beginning of a rare happening: he became an expert in suggesting medication for incurable diseases; during his life he cured some thirty thousand people. Whatever prescription he gave was always right; without exception, every patient who tried his medication was cured – but Cayce himself was not able to explain it. He could only say that whenever he closed his eyes to look for some treatment, his eyes would turn upward as if pulled toward the middle of his eyebrows. His eyes became fixed there and he forgot everything; he only remembered that after a certain point he became oblivious to his surroundings, and until he arrived at that point the treatment would not come to him. He suggested some wonderful remedies, two of which are worth understanding.

The Rothschilds were a very rich family in America. A woman from that family had been sick for a long time and no treatment had helped. Then she was brought to Edgar Cayce, and in his unconscious state he suggested a certain medication. We have to call his state unconscious, but those who know about this mysterious happening would say he was fully conscious at that time. In fact, unconsciousness continues until our knowing reaches to the level of the third eye.

Rothschild was a millionaire, so he could afford to search the whole of America for this medication, but he could not find it. No one could even say whether this medication actually existed. Advertisements were placed in international newspapers requesting information about it. After almost three weeks a man from Sweden wrote, saying there was no medication of that name in existence – although twenty years earlier his father had patented a medication under that name, but never had it manufactured. He wrote that his father had died, but he could send the formula. The medication was then made up and given to the woman, who recovered. How could Cayce have known of a drug that had not even been available on the market?

In another incident, he again suggested a particular medicine to someone: a search was made for it, but it could not be found. A year later an advertisement appeared in a newspaper announcing the availability of this medicine. During the previous year it had been in the process of being tested in the laboratories; it had not even been given a name, but Cayce had known of it. The medicine was then given to the patient, who soon recovered.

Cayce had also suggested medicines which could not be found, and these patients died. When he was asked about this, he said he was helpless, but there was nothing he could do. He said, 'I do not know who is seeing these things and who is speaking when I am unconscious – I have no relationship to the person.' But one thing was certain: whenever he was speaking in this state his eyes were drawn upward.

When we are in deep sleep, our eyes are drawn upward relative to the depth of our sleep. Now, psychologists are experimenting a great deal on sleep. The deeper you are in sleep, the higher your eyes are; the lower the eyes, the greater is their movement. If your eyes are moving very rapidly under their eyelids, you are having a very eventful dream. Now it has been scientifically proved by thorough experiments that rapid eye movement, REM, indicates a fast-moving dream. The lower the eyes, the greater the REM; as the eyes go higher, the REM is reduced. When the REM is zero, sleep is at its deepest. At that point the eyes remain steadily fixed between the two eyebrows.

Yoga says that in deep sleep we reach the same state that we reach in deep meditation. The place where the eyes become fixed is the same in deep sleep as *in deep meditation*.

I have told you about these two historical events only to indicate there is a point between your two eyebrows where this worldly life ceases, and the life of the other world begins – that point is a door. On this side of the door, this world flourishes, and on the other side there is an unknown, supernatural world.

The *tilak*, the vermilion mark on the forehead, was first devised as an indication and symbol of that unknown world. It cannot be applied just anywhere, and only one who can place his hand on the forehead and find the point can tell you where to apply the *tilak*. There is no use in putting the *tilak* just anywhere because the point is not in exactly the same place on everyone. The third eye is not found in the same place on everyone; it is somewhere above the middle of the two eyebrows on most people. If someone has meditated for a long time in his past lives and has had a small experience of samadhi, his third eye will be lower down. If no meditation has been done, the place on the forehead is higher up. It can be determined by the position of this point what the state of your meditation was in your past life; it will indicate whether the state of samadhi ever happened to you in your past life. If it happened often, this point will have come down lower, it will be at the same level as your eyes – it cannot go lower than that. If this point has come in line with your eyes, then with just the smallest happening one can enter samadhi. In fact, the happening can be so small it can appear to be insignificant. And so often we are surprised when someone appears to slip into samadhi without an apparent cause.

There is a story about a Zen nun. She was returning with a pot of water on her head after fetching water from a well. The pot somehow fell, and in that falling the woman achieved became enlightened. The incident seems so insignificant: the pot falls and breaks – and enlightenment happens! There seems to be no logical connection.

There is another such event, this one in the life of Lao Tzu. He was sitting under a tree during autumn and the dry leaves of the tree were falling. Watching them, Lao Tzu became enlightened.

There is no relationship between enlightenment and leaves falling, but such things happen when – because of work done in past lives – your spiritual journey is almost completed and the third-eye point has moved down so it is between your two eyes. Then any small happening will tip the scales, and that final small happening can be anything.

If the vermillion or sandal-paste mark is put just at the right spot, it indicates several things. Firstly, if your master has told you to wear a *tilak* on a particular spot, you will begin to experience something there. You may not have thought about this, but if you sit with closed eyes and someone closely points his finger at the spot between your two eyes, you will have the feeling someone is pointing his finger at you. This is the perception of the third eye.

If the *tilak* is the same size as your third eye and it is put at just the right place, you will remember that place for twenty-four hours and forget the rest of the body. This remembering will make you more aware of the *tilak* and less of your body. Then a moment comes when nothing else is remembered about the body except the *tilak*. When that happens, you will be able to open your third eye. In this practice, as you forget the body and just remember the *tilak*, your whole consciousness crystallizes and becomes focused on the third eye. The key that opens the third eye is focused consciousness. It is just like focusing the rays of the sun on a piece of paper with the help of a lens – you create enough heat to burn the paper. When those sunrays are concentrated, fire is produced. When consciousness remains spread all over the whole body, it is just doing the work of carrying on your life, but when it becomes totally focused on the third eye, the barrier to seeing with the third eye is burned, and the door which allows you to see the inner sky is opened.

So the first use of the *tilak* is to show you the right place on the body so you remember it twenty-four hours a day. Another use of the *tilak* is to make it easier for the master to see the place without having to put his hand on your forehead to see your progress – because as the place moves downward, you will put the *tilak* a little lower. Each day you have to feel the place and move the *tilak* to it, to where you feel the presence of the third eye.

The master may have thousands of disciples: while the disciple bows down to him, the master observes where his *tilak* is and does not need to ask anything about his progress. The *tilak* indicates whether the disciple is making progress, or whether he is obstructed by something and has become stuck. If the disciple cannot feel the downward movement of the spot, it means he is not totally focusing his consciousness. And if he has put the *tilak* on the wrong place, it means he is not conscious of the exact point.

As the point goes on moving downward, the methods of meditation will have to be changed. The *tilak* is to the master what a patient's progress chart is to the doctor in a hospital. The nurse goes on recording the temperature, blood pressure, pulse, and so on; the doctor just has to see the chart to know the patient's condition. Similarly, the *tilak* was a great experiment to indicate the condition of the disciple – the master had no need to ask anything. He knew what help was needed or what needed to be changed. This was the value of the *tilak* – assessing the changes needed in meditation.

Another aspect of the third eye is that it is the center of willpower. In Yoga it is called the *agya* chakra. We call it that because whatever discipline we have in our life is governed by it; whatever order and harmony there is in our life arises from this point.

Let us understand it this way: all of us have a sex center, and it is easier to understand through the sex center because we are all aware of it – we are not very aware of the third-eye chakra. All our desires in life are born at the sex center. As long as the sex center is not activated, there is no sexual desire. However, every child is born with the capacity for sex and the entire mechanism for fulfilling sexual desire.

It is a strange fact that women are born with all the egg cells they could need for the entire length of their reproductive life. Not a single new egg cell can be produced later. From the first day of her life, the number of eggs a woman has indicates the potential number of children she can give birth to. After she reaches puberty, every month one egg cell will be released from her ovaries. If it meets and unites with a sperm from a man's semen, a child is conceived. Then no more eggs are released as long as that embryo is developing, and until after the newborn child is a few months old.

The desire for sex, however, does not arise until the sex center becomes active. As long as this center is inactive, even though the necessary equipment for sex is complete in the body, sexual desire is not aroused. When one reaches the age of thirteen or fourteen, this center becomes active. We know this center because although we are not activating it, it becomes activated by nature. If the situation were otherwise, very few people would become aware of it. Have you ever wondered why, if just a thought of sex passes through your mind, the whole reproductive system becomes active? The thought arises in the mind – faraway from the sex center, but the thought immediately activates the sex center. Every idea or thought about sex draws the sex center toward itself. Every thought is attracted toward its relative center, just as water flows to the lowest level.

The third-eye center is the center of willpower. Let us understand what its function is.

People whose third-eye chakra is not activated in this life will remain slaves in thousands of ways. Without this center there is no freedom. We know about political and economic freedom, but these freedoms are not real – a person who has no willpower, whose third-eye chakra is not activated, will always remain a slave in one way or another. He may become free from one kind of slavery, but he will become a slave to something else. He does not have a center of will to make him the master of himself, he has no willpower. He does not have the power to command himself; his body and senses command him. If his stomach says it is hungry, he is hungry. If his body says it is sick, he becomes sick. If his sex center says he needs sex, the sexual desire arises. If his body says it has become old, he becomes old. The body commands and he obeys.

But as soon as the center of willpower becomes activated, the body stops giving orders and instead it starts to obey; the whole arrangement is reversed. If such a person asks his blood to stop flowing, it will; if he asks his heart to stop beating, it will. He can ask his pulse to stop throbbing and it will. Such a person becomes the master of his body, mind, and senses, but without the activation of the third-eye chakra, this cannot be. The more you bring awareness to this center, the more you become the master of yourself.

Many experiments have been done in Yoga to awaken this center. Wearing a *tilak* on the forehead is one of them. If sombody bring his awareness to this center every now and then, there will be great results. If a *tilak* is put there, your attention is repeatedly drawn there. As soon as the *tilak* is put on, the spot becomes set apart from the rest of your body. This spot is very sensitive, and if the *tilak* is on the right spot you will have to remember it. It is possibly the most sensitive spot in the body. It was an attempt to touch this sensitivity.

There are methods for marking this sensitive spot. After hundreds of experiments, sandalwood paste was chosen. There is a sort of resonance between sandalwood paste and the sensitivity of the third-eye chakra, and if applied on that spot the paste deepens its sensitivity. Not just any substance can be used; some other substances, in fact, can badly damage the sensitivity of that spot.

For example, women stick a colored plastic dot on their foreheads, but these *tikas* from the marketplace do not have any scientific basis. They have nothing to do with Yoga, and they cause harm to the sensitivity of the third eye. The question is whether a substance increases the sensitivity of the spot or decreases it. If it increases the sensitivity, it is good; otherwise, it is harmful. In this world even a small thing can make a whole lot of difference; everything has its own separate effect. Keeping this in mind, some special things were found to be useful. If the third-eye chakra can become sensitive and be activated, it will bring about an increased integrity and dignity in you. You will begin to be more integrated, whole; everything inside you ceases to be separate and divided and you become whole.

There is a small difference between the use of the *tika*, the small round mark and the *tilak*, a longer mark. The *tika* was meant particularly for women. In women, the third-eye chakra is very weak, it has to be because the woman's entire personality is created for surrender – her beauty is in surrender. If her third-eye chakra becomes powerful, then surrendering will be difficult. Her third-eye chakra is weak, very weak compared to a man's – that is why a woman always needs someone's help in one form or another. She does not ordinarily venture to stand on her own, but looks to a helping hand, someone's shoulder to lean on, someone to lead her. She likes someone to tell her to do something, and her willingness to follow makes her happy.

India is the only country in which an attempt has been made to activate the woman's third-eye chakra. This is only because it was felt that unless the third-eye chakra is activated, the woman will not be able to make any progress in spiritual life; without willpower she cannot make any progress in meditative practices. It has to be made sound and strong, but it is necessary to make her third-eye chakra strong in a different way because if it is done in the usual way, the same way as for a man, it will reduce her femininity and she will begin to develop the qualities of a man.

So the *tika* was invariably and firmly associated with a woman's husband. This association was needed because if it was just applied independently, it would increase a woman's independence and make her self-sufficient. And the more independent she became, the more her delicateness, her beauty and flexibility would be destroyed. There is a tenderness and softness in her seeking help from others, but if she became independent she would not be able to avoid becoming hard and rigid. So it was thought that to make her strong directly would damage her femininity, it would create problems for her being a mother; it would make it difficult for her to surrender. Hence an effort was made to associate her will center with her husband. This was helpful; her femininity would not be affected, but her will center would still become activated.

Let us understand it this way: the third-eye chakra cannot go against the person who it is associated with. If it is associated with the religious master, it cannot go against him. If it is associated with a woman's husband, she can never go against him either. If a *tika* is put on the right spot on a woman's forehead, with its deep association with her husband, she will follow him, but at the same time she will be powerful in relating with the rest of the world.

If you understand what hypnotism is, you will be able to understand this associative phenomenon. If a hypnotist hypnotizes someone, then the hypnotized person will be able to hear only the voice of the hypnotist. He will hear the quiet command of the hypnotist, but he will not hear any loud noises that may be created by the spectators. This is similar to what happens when an Indian woman wears a *tika*: it makes her deeply suggestible. The hypnotized person remains open only to the hypnotist and closed to everyone else. If the hypnotist even whispers for the person to stand up, the person will do it, but he will not hear anyone else's loud command. This person's consciousness has now only one opening, toward the hypnotist, his third-eye chakra has become tied up only with the hypnotist.

This mantra is used in connection with the woman's *tika*. She will follow only her husband and surrender herself only to him. She maintains her freedom and independence toward the rest of the world, but now there will be no problem with her femininity; her womanhood can be preserved, her feminine qualities are left undisturbed. When the husband dies, the *tika* has to be removed because now she is not to follow anybody. People have no idea about the scientific approach regarding the *tika*, they think that the *tika* is removed because a woman has become a widow – but there is a reason for removing it. Now she will have to live like any man for the rest of her life; and the more independent she becomes, the better it will be. Even the slightest area of vulnerability which might cause her to follow someone has to be closed.

This *tika* experiment was very deep: but it has to be on the right spot and of the right material and put on correctly, otherwise it is meaningless. If the *tika* is only decorative it has no value. Then it is only a formality. So when the *tika* is applied to a woman for the first time, it is done with ceremony, and with a formal ritual in the same way that a master puts a *tilak* on the disciple's forehead for the first time. Only if it is done that way will it be effective, and not otherwise.

Now all these things have become meaningless because the entire chain of scientific thinking behind them has been lost. It has become just an empty ritual, a hollow outer shell that is somehow still being carried, without any purpose, without any love.

I will tell you a few more things about the third-eye chakra which will be useful. The line drawn upward from the *agya* chakra divides the brain in two: right and left; the brain begins at that line. It has been observed that half our brain is not utilized: the most intelligent people among us – our geniuses – also use barely half of the brain, and the remaining half is unused and undeveloped. Scientists and psychologists are puzzled as to why this is so. Even if that half of the brain were to be surgically removed, everything would continue to function normally; the person would not even know that half of his brain has been removed. Scientists know that nature does not create anything unnecessarily – there could be a mistake with one person's brain, but not with the brains of the whole of humanity! But in all humans half of the brain is unused, inactive, without any movement whatsoever.

Yoga maintains that this half of the brain becomes active only after the third-eye chakra is activated. Half of the brain is connected with the centers below the third-eye chakra, and the other half is connected with the centers above the third-eye chakra. When the centers below the third-eye chakra are working, the left side of the brain is utilized. When the centers above it begin to work, the right side of the brain is activated. As long as there is no experience of the activities of that other half, there can be no conception of it.

In Sweden, a man fell from a train. When he was taken to the hospital, he began hearing the programs which were being broadcast on radio stations within a ten-mile radius around him. At first it was thought there was some damage to his brain because he was describing the sound as just a humming in his ears, but after two weeks he began to hear the radio programs clearly, and he became very frightened and asked the doctor what was wrong. He told the doctor he could hear the radio programs as clearly as if he had a radio near his ears. The doctor asked him what he was hearing, and he repeated the line of a song; the doctor had just heard that particular song on the radio at his home from where he had just come. After that song, the radio transmission for that session had stopped and the doctor had left for the hospital. When the transmission began again, a radio was brought into the hospital to compare what the patient heard with what was being transmitted. It was found that this man's ears were functioning like a radio receiver. Eventually he had to be operated on; otherwise he would have gone mad because there was no way to switch off the programs. He could hear the broadcasts all the time, whether he wanted to or not.

This incident made one thing clear – that the ear has a great potential. By the turn of this century it may be possible to use our ears to listen to broadcasts directly. The ear could work like a radio receiver simply by attaching an on-off switch near the ear! The idea only came because this man had a train accident. Many new inventions have been made and new ideas and perspectives have arisen accidentally in this world. On the basis of our past knowledge we could never have thought that someday our ears might act as radio receivers. Both the ear and the radio receiver do the work of hearing – both are receptive – but the radio was made after the ear, the ear served as a model: the radio is meaningful only because of our ears. The other potentialities of the ears will not be known unless we happen to accidentally stumble on them.

A similar incident happened during the Second World War. A man was wounded and became unconscious. When he regained consciousness, he began to see stars in the sky in the daytime. Stars are always there, but because of the radiance of the sun we are not able to see them during the day; they are very far away and the sunlight intervenes.

There are stars which are hundreds and thousands of times bigger and brighter than the sun, but they are farther away from the earth than the sun. Sunrays take about 9 minutes to reach the earth, whereas the light from the nearest star takes 4 years to reach the earth. The light from the sun travels at the speed of 186,000 miles per second. Even at this speed, sunlight takes about 9 minutes to reach the earth – and light from the nearest star takes 4 years. There are stars so far away that their light might take 4,000 years, 400,000 years, 40,000,000 years, or 4,000,000,000 years to reach the earth. Some scientists say there are stars whose light rays began traveling toward the earth before it was born and may only reach here by the time the earth has disappeared. Those light rays may never know there was a phenomenon called earth that existed during their journey.

The stars that this wounded man saw do exist during the day, they just cannot be seen – but he saw them. What happened to his eyes? – they had developed an extraordinary capacity. This incident revealed the potential of the eyes; it indicated there is dormant potential in our eyes, of which we are unaware – all our senses have great dormant potential. Whatever seems like a miracle to us is only because of the sudden revelation of some of our ordinarily dormant potential; it is not a miracle. There are many miracles within us that are not manifest; they are hidden behind locked doors.

Just a few minutes ago I was telling you that half of the brain usually remains unused, and only becomes active when the third-eye chakra becomes activated – that is the insight of Yoga. Such insights have not just come to light from recent experience, but have been known for at least twenty thousand years. You cannot rely on any conclusion reached by science because what science believes to be true today may be proved wrong within six months, but these insights of Yoga are confirmed by the experience of at least twenty thousand years. We have the illusion that ours is the first civilization, but many human civilizations have happened before and have vanished. Many times before us man reached the same or higher heights of scientific progress, but those civilizations were destroyed.

In 1924, a center for research in atomic science was established in Germany. Suddenly one morning, someone, giving his name as Falkaneli, went to the institute and handed in a written message to the center authorities. In the letter he had written, 'I and a few others know certain facts about atomic science, and on the basis of that knowledge, I warn you not to go ahead with your atomic research because before our civilization, many others destroyed themselves through explosive atomic energy. It is better to stop any further research.' Afterward, efforts were made to find the writer, but without success.

In 1940, Heisenberg, a very great scientist in Germany, had been working to develop atomic energy. Again, the same person, Falkaneli, came to his house, handed a note to his servant, and then went away. The note contained the same message, and again the author could not be traced.

In 1945, when the atomic bomb was dropped on Hiroshima, all twelve scientists who had helped to make the atomic bomb were sent a similar letter by Falkaneli, telling them that even now it was not too late to stop further development of their work. Otherwise, since the first step toward destruction had been taken, the last step was not far off. Oppenheimer – who was the greatest American nuclear scientist, and who had also contributed a great deal toward the making of the atomic bomb – immediately resigned from the nuclear board after receiving this letter and issued a statement saying, 'We have sinned' – but once more this Falkaneli could not be traced. What Falkaneli was saying is very possible: earlier civilizations did play with atomic power and did destroy themselves.

In India, at the time of the Mahabharata war, we also played with atomic energy and destroyed ourselves. This is the situation: a child becomes a young man and commits the same mistakes which his father committed. The father, who is now old, warns him not to – in his own time, his father had also warned him – but in youth such mistakes are committed, although the younger generations are warned by those who meanwhile have become old. Civilizations are also destroyed by taking the same steps, and making mistakes similar to those of past civilizations. Civilizations, too, pass through childhood and youth, and then become old and die.

The insights of Yoga have been gained over a period of twenty thousand years – historically, the calculations for a period of twenty thousand years are fairly clear. If you want to study the youth of one man, you need to study that of ten – because what is true for one man, may not be true for all men. The study of a single person and a single event are not conclusive enough by themselves, so that is why I said the picture of the past twenty thousand years is fairly clear.

For twenty thousand years, Yoga has maintained that if you want to know what there is beyond this worldly life, you have to activate the other half of the brain connected to the dormant and inactive third eye. If you want to know anything about the absolute, that which is beyond matter, this other half of the brain will have to be activated. And the door to this half of the brain – the place of the third-eye chakra – is where we apply the *tilak*. That spot is the outward location, and it corresponds to the inner center, which is about one and a half inches inside the forehead. That deep point, that center, functions as a door to that transcendental world beyond matter.

Just as in India the *tilak* was devised, in Tibet methods were devised of actually surgically operating on this spot in order to reach the third-eye chakra. Tibetans have made a lot of effort to find the third eye, more than any other civilization. In fact all of Tibet's sciences and understanding about life in its various aspects are based on the understanding of the third eye.

I told you earlier about Edgar Cayce giving prescriptions while in a trance. He was the only such case in America, but in Tibet people would ask for medical advice only from those who were able to go into trance, into samadhi. Tibetans tried to reach the third-eye chakra surgically, by breaking it open from the outside, but reaching this place surgically is quite different from reaching it internally through Yoga practices, as has been done in India. When the dormant half of the brain becomes activated internally through Yoga practices, it becomes activated because of the development of consciousness. Opening this center from the outside, without any refining or purifying of consciousness, creates the danger that the achievements of that half of the brain may be misused after it has been activated –

because the man remains the same, his consciousness has not been transformed from within through meditation. What is needed is a change in consciousness through meditation.

If this half of the brain becomes activated without an inner transformation, then for example, the person who becomes capable of seeing through walls and beyond material obstructions may not try to save someone whom he sees has fallen into a well, but he may prefer to dig out treasures which he can see lying hidden under the ground. If such a person realizes that he can make people obey him, he might order you to do things to benefit himself.

External operations could have been done in India also, but Indians never attempted to do them because practitioners of Yoga know that if consciousness is not transformed from within, it is dangerous to activate such powers and put them in the hands of people who might misuse them. It is like giving a sword to a child. He may not only kill other people, he might also kill himself. So a transformation of consciousness is necessary before new powers are activated.

In Tibet, they tried to make a hole with physical instruments on the spot where we apply the *tilak*, so Tibetans came to know and experience many of the powers of the dormant brain, but – as far as spiritual discipline is concerned – Tibet could not become a great country. It is surprising that even though Tibet did a great deal, it could not give birth to a Buddha. It developed many powers, it came to know many unique things, but it used them for trivial matters.

India did not try to experiment with physical instruments, but tried to concentrate and focus the total energy on the third-eye chakra from within, so the third eye would open by the very force of that surging energy. It is a great discipline to bring the flow of consciousness up to the third eye; the mind has to be elevated to high levels of discipline. Normally, the mind gravitates downward, in fact our mind normally flows toward the sex center. Whatever we may be doing – earning money, increasing our status, anything – in a subtle way, it is our desire for sex that is the motivating force. If we are earning money, it is only in the hope we can buy sex. We seek higher positions only in order to be powerful enough to be able to select and secure sexual partners.

That is why, in days past, the reputation of a king was measured by the number of queens he had. And that is the right measure, because what *is* the value of your power? So, power, status, and money are in a roundabout way only meant for the satisfaction of that fundamental sex drive. As long as your energies are flowing downward, toward the sex center, it is possible you will be spiritually undisciplined.

If you want to direct your energy to higher levels, then the direction of your sexual energy will have to be reversed. The entire direction of the flow has to be changed. You will have to make an about-face, and shift your entire attention to an upward direction. There must be an upward vertical movement – and this will be a great spiritual discipline. At every step there will be confrontation and a need for sacrifices. You will have to lose all that is inferior and lower in order to gain that which is vast and sublime. This price has to be paid. And when you achieve higher powers at such a cost, how can you then misuse them? There is no question of misuse because the person who was capable of misusing these powers will be finished before he reaches the goal.

It is because of this that black magic was born in Tibet – because of those external operations. There was very little spiritual growth, and evil practices could thrive due to the immense powers that became available.

Among Sufis there is a story about Jesus; in Christianity there is no mention of this anywhere, but there are many such stories about Jesus among the Sufis, stories which Christianity does not have. Even Moslems have accounts of some important events in the life of Jesus which are not found in Christianity.

This story is recorded by the Sufis . . .

Jesus had three disciples who said to him they had heard about his power to revive the dead. They did not want salvation or the Kingdom of God, but they wanted him to tell them the secret of raising the dead, so they could have that power. Jesus told them they would never be able to use the mantra for themselves because once they were dead, how could they use it? How would they benefit in making others come to life? He told them instead he would show them how to not die at all, but the disciples said they were not worried about their own deaths, they were only interested in knowing how the dead could be made alive.

Finally Jesus became tired of them and he showed them the method. Immediately all three left him to search for a dead body somewhere, to try out the mantra before they forgot something or made some mistake. Unfortunately, in the first village they reached they could not find a dead body, so they went to another one, and on the way they found a skeleton. As they could not find a dead body, they thought they would try the mantra on the skeleton. It was the skeleton of a lion. They used the mantra and immediately the lion came to life, and killed all three of them!

Sufis say that only such things can be the result – the curiosity of an unethical mind can take one into great danger. And so, much secret knowledge was kept hidden so it could not fall into the wrong hands. Anything given to an ordinary person was given in such a way that they would come to understand it only when they deserved to.

You may wonder why I have been telling you all this in relation to the *tilak*. A *tilak* was put on every child's forehead when he did not understand anything about it, but as he grew up and came to understand such things, he would figure out the mystery of the *tilak*. Until then, just a hint about the right spot was given. Whenever the child's consciousness became capable, he could make use of this mark. It did not even matter if out of a hundred people, only one became capable of using the *tilak*; that one was enough. If it made only one person aware of his third-eye center it had served its purpose.

There is so much value placed on the *tilak* that on all special occasions, such as marriage or victory, the *tilak* is applied. Have you ever stopped to wonder why the *tilak* is applied on every occasion of respect and honor? It is because of the law of association. Our mind is very interesting. It wants to forget the moments of misery and wants to remember the moments of happiness. That is why the mind forgets all events that brought unhappiness and remembers only the moments that gave happiness. That is why we always feel that the past was full of happiness. An old man always thinks he was happy in his childhood. It is because the mind drops all painful memories, and keeps those that are pleasant. So when a person looks back on the past, he only sees happiness. Whatever unhappiness was there in between the pleasant moments is forgotten.

No child ever says his childhood is full of happiness. Children want to grow up fast: it is old people who say their childhood was full of happiness – there is a misunderstanding somewhere. If you ask a child what he would like, he will tell you he wants to grow up. If you ask old people what they want, they will say they would like to be children again. The child always tries to look grown-up and tries to become older. He begins to smoke cigarettes only because he feels that smoking is a symbol of being grown up. Psychologists say that seventy percent of children begin smoking because it is a symbol of prestige. They think only big, strong, successful people smoke.

So when a child smokes, he holds himself straight and he feels he is somebody – not just an ordinary person.

If a film is 'For adults only', boys will put on fake moustaches to try to get into the show – why? There is a burning desire in children to grow up quickly, yet old people say that childhood was very happy – why? The only reason is that the mind makes us forget unhappy times; unhappiness is not worth remembering.

One psychologist, Piaget, after experimenting with children for forty years, found that the memory of the first five years of life is very poor, almost nil – because those years are so unhappy the child does not want to remember them. If you try to remember the events of your early life, according to Piaget you will remember back to when you were five, or at the most four years old. Was there no memory formation before then? There was. Were there no events before you were five years old? There were. In those early days did no one abuse you? Did someone not love you? All these things happened, but why then is there no memory of those first four or five years?

Piaget says that early childhood days were full of unhappiness for the child: the child feels weak, helpless, and so dependent that he suppresses the memory, he simply drops those days from his memory. If asked about them, he simply says, 'I don't remember anything before the age of four' because when his father told him to get up, he had to obey; if his mother told him to sit down, he had to obey. Everyone around him was more powerful and he could not go against them – he was as helpless as a dry leaf in the wind. He had to do whatever he was told; he was dependent on others for everything. Just the hint of anger in the other's eye and he was frightened.

So he just closes up and forgets that he had any life before he was four years old. But if he is hypnotized, and asked to remember events from before he was four, or even when he was in his mother's womb, he will remember and describe them. If during the pregnancy his mother fell over, under the influence of hypnosis the child can remember the shock it felt in her womb – but in ordinary consciousness usually such memories cannot be recalled.

There is a strong reason to associate the *tilak* with one's moments of happiness. Whenever there is a happy event, let a tilak be put on your forehead. Both the happy event and the *tilak* will be remembered through association. Here it is necessary to know a little about the law of association.

Pavlov, the Russian scientist, carried out many experiments in this area. He said anything can be associated with anything else – our lives are just the sum total of our associations. One of his experiments is well-known. It involved offering food to a dog. Pavlov would put the food at some distance, so the dog would start salivating while he was looking at the food. Then Pavlov would ring a bell. There is no connection between a bell and the secretion of saliva, but whenever the food was offered to the dog, the secretion of saliva would begin and then the bell was rung. This was done for fifteen days, and so the mental association between the bell and the saliva was established. On the sixteenth day there was no food, but when the bell was rung the dog began to salivate. The ringing of the bell activated the dog's memory of the food: the bell became a symbol for the food.

This same law of association has been used with the *tilak*: it has become associated with happiness. Whenever a happy event occurred, a *tilak* was used – so gradually the *tilak* and happiness became so associated that the *tilak* could never be forgotten. So whenever you become happy, you will first remember the third-eye chakra. We always like to remember happy moments, and whether we were really happy or not, we live in happy memories. Even small happinesses are exaggerated; we magnify the happy events and minimize the unhappy ones.

When you first met your beloved, you were so happy! When you think about it today, it was such a great event, but when you actually meet her today, that happiness will have shrunk. Then again within the next twenty-four hours you will magnify it. There is so much unhappiness in life: if we did not magnify the happiness it would be difficult to live.

If the *tilak* is associated with happiness, as the happiness becomes magnified, so too does the *tilak*. When this happens frequently, happiness becomes associated with the third-eye chakra. When this happens, you must realize that you have used happiness in order to open the third eye. We can use this stream of happiness to activate the third-eye chakra. The more we activate it from different directions, the more helpful it is.

The countries which have not used the *tilak* have not known what the third eye is. Countries which had even the slightest inkling of the third eye have made use of the *tilak*. The countries which had no concept of the third eye could not invent the *tilak*: there was no basis for it. A society will not suddenly get the idea of applying a *tilak* to the forehead without any reason; there is no reason to apply a *tilak* just at random on any spot. So it is not just accidental, and such a practice can survive only if there is a deep reason for it.

I will tell you a few more things about this third-eye point. You may have noticed that whenever you are anxious there is a pressure on your third eye – because of that your forehead contracts and wrinkles are formed. The tension builds up just on the spot where the *tilak* would be placed. Those who are continuously tense, and constantly thinking and reflecting, can invariably indicate the location of the spot by the pressure which they feel on their forehead.

People who have worked hard on the third eye in their past lives have, at the time of birth, a sort of *tilak* on the forehead right at the third-eye point. This spot appears slightly worn, just as if a *tilak* had been there. If you touch this spot on the forehead with your finger, it will feel a little swollen – just there, where in past lives a *tilak* was worn. Behind a *tilak* or *tika* is hidden the third eye.

There was a small experiment carried out by hypnotists: Charcot was a great psychologist in France, who worked on the subject of influencing a person by focusing his eyes on the other's forehead. If you try to concentrate your gaze on someone's forehead, he will become very angry and will not let you continue. It is thought ill-mannered and rude to do so. From the forehead the third-eye chakra is about one and a half inches inside – very close to the surface. If someone is walking in front of you, and you fix your eyes on the back of his head, approximately at the level of his third-eye spot, you will find that, within a few seconds, this person will turn to look around behind him. If you continue this experiment for a few days and then give someone some suggestions, he will carry them out.

Try to understand: if you focus your gaze at the back of his head for a few seconds, without even once letting your eyelids close, the person will look behind him. Then just at that moment, you can mentally command him to do something. If you ask him to turn left he will do so, although he will feel very embarrassed – he may have wanted to turn right. If you do this experiment for some time, you will be surprised at the results. From the back of the head the distance to the third-eye point is further than from the front, where the distance is only one and a half inches – and from the front the results are even more surprising.

People who practice fake *shaktipat*, transmitting energy, are able to do so through the third-eye chakra. If some holy man or monk makes you sit in front of him with your eyes closed, you may think he is really doing something – he is only fixing his eyes on this spot on your forehead and mentally giving you a suggestion. If he says, 'There is bright light within you,' you will feel there is light inside you, but that light does not remain with you – as soon as you are away from him it vanishes. Sometimes that illusion of light may persist for two or three days, and then it dies out. It is not genuine *shaktipat*, but only an insignificant exercise on your third-eye chakra.

The third eye is a unique gift, and there are innumerable uses for it.

When Christian missionaries came to southern India for the first time, some of them began applying the *tilak* to their foreheads. Because of this, about a thousand years ago, a situation arose in the Vatican court in which an explanation was demanded from those missionaries in India. Some of them had begun to wear the sacred thread, some had applied the *tilak*, and some even wore wooden sandals on their feet – they had begun to live like Hindu sannyasins.

The Vatican court felt that these missionaries were doing something wrong. The missionaries who had begun to live in this way in India replied they were not becoming Hindus by applying the *tilak*, but that by doing so they had come to know a secret. By wearing wooden sandals on their feet they had not become Hindus, but they had come to know that if they wore wooden sandals while meditating, the energy does not get dissipated and so results that would have taken months without the wooden sandals came about within a short time. They also said that if Hindus have come to know certain secrets, Christian missionaries would only be fools not to learn them.

Certainly Hindus know many things – it would be really surprising if they did not, having been on a religious quest for twenty thousand years. For twenty thousand years all their most intelligent and wisest men have devoted their lives to the same end – the search for truth. They were possessed with only one desire: to know the truth that is hidden behind this existence, to see that which is invisible, and to encounter that which is formless. It would be really amazing if such people did not know anything, after having single-mindedly dedicated all their intelligence to this single quest for twenty thousand years continuously. It is only natural they would know – and they do! But during the last two hundred years, certain things happened which are very disturbing.

It is worth understanding. In this country there have been hundreds of foreign invasions, but no invader could ever attack the vital core. Some invaders looked for wealth, some occupied land, others captured palaces and forts, but none could attack the interiority of India – the attention of invaders was not drawn toward it. But then, for the first time, attacks were made on its interiority by Western civilization. The easiest way to attack it was to disconnect the country from its long history, and to destroy the past. A gap was created between the people and their history. In this way people became uprooted and powerless.

If Western civilization were to be destroyed today, there would be no need to destroy its buildings, its cinemas, its theaters, or its hotels. If just the five most famous universities were destroyed, all of Western culture would disappear. Western culture does not reside in its cinemas, hotels, or night clubs – it makes no difference if they continue – but if the most eminent universities were destroyed, Western civilization would slowly die and become lost. The real basis of all cultures is its sources of knowledge. The roots of a civilization are in its long chain of knowledge. If the history of just two generations were taken away, a country would become cut off from all possibilities of further progress.

That is the difference between human beings and animals. Animals are not able to make progress because they do not have schools. They have no way to transfer knowledge from the older generation to the new generation. At its birth, an animal begins life right from where its father began, and its offspring will do the same. The human being, through education, can help his child's life to begin from where he left off. So there is a continuity of knowledge. All human progress depends on the transfer of accumulated knowledge from generation to generation.

Just imagine if for twenty years all adults decided not to teach anything to their children. It would not just be a loss of twenty years' worth of knowledge, but all the knowledge which has been collected over twenty thousand years could become lost. And such a loss could not be made up for in twenty years: it would take twenty thousand years to make up the gap because a discontinuity would have been created in the accumulation of knowledge.

In this way, the two hundred years of British dominance in India created a great gap. Most of its links with the ancient knowledge and wisdom were broken, and it had to establish an identity with a totally new civilization and culture with which its older civilization had no relationship. Indians think theirs is a very old civilization, but they are mistaken – they are only a two-hundred-year-old community. The British are now a far older community than the Indians. Whatever knowledge India has now is just rubbish, and that too is just leftovers. That which the West chooses to give India now is its knowledge. Whatever India knew before two hundred years ago was lost in one stroke.

When the threads of a branch of knowledge are lost, people seem just like ignorant fools. If you go out now with a *tika* on your forehead, and someone asks you why you are wearing it, you will feel ashamed because you have no answer. You can only say, 'No reason. My father insisted on my doing it, and so I had to. What to do? Certain things have to be put up with.' So these days, applying a *tika* cheerfully is difficult, if not impossible. Of course, a simpleton can do it – he has no fear of others – but he is doing it not because he knows its purpose, but because he has been told to.

When the links of real knowledge are broken, the outward symbols of it become difficult to carry. Then a certain tragedy results: those with intelligence keep away. And a thing remains meaningful only as long as intelligent people are involved in it. So it is interesting to note that whenever such a misfortune overwhelms a civilization, whenever it loses its connection with past knowledge, the intellectuals drift away from it because they do not like to look foolish. And the ignorant masses try to preserve the symbols and follow the rituals, and so those symbols and rituals will continue for some time and then die a natural death.

So sometimes it happens that some valuable things are preserved by ignorant and backward people. And the people who claim to understand disappear at the first opportunity. Life is very complex.

If India wants to restore the broken links with its past, people will have to look at every ritual being performed by the ignorant and illiterate masses. What they are doing is not without reason. Their outward symbols are linked with a past of twenty thousand years. They may not be able to explain why they are doing certain things, but there is no need to frown upon them. Some day we may have to thank them for at least having saved the symbols of that knowledge – symbols on which research can be done.

So in India today, what these illiterate people are doing needs to be reconnected with the knowledge we had prior to two hundred years ago. Only by doing that can we revive and give new life to the deep understanding that grew over a period of twenty thousand years. Then we will be surprised at how suicidal we have been.

4
The Transformative Power of Idols

Doctor Frank Rudolf spent his whole life doing research on an amazing phenomenon. I would like to tell you about it, so that you can understand more easily what idol worship is about. Rudolf studied and reached surprising conclusions about a particular process that most primitive communities have been familiar with for a long time.

Certain primitive tribes believe that it is possible to make a person suffer from a particular disease through a clay effigy that represents him. They believe that even death can be brought about in this way. Doctor Rudolf spent thirty years trying to find out how it is possible to transmit disease and death through an earthen representation of someone. Rudolf lived amongst the tribes in the Amazon for years, and approached the subject skeptically and scientifically. Hundreds of times he actually saw disease and death being transmitted with his own eyes, even if the person was a thousand miles away.

His long study convinced him of the truth of such happenings. There were three things which he came to understand after all his experiments: firstly, it was not necessary for the clay effigy to exactly resemble the person in whom disease or death was to be invoked. It is difficult even for an experienced sculptor to make a clay effigy which is exactly like a particular person, but it is not necessary. What is important is to establish the shape and form of the person mentally on the earthen representation. And there is a method for doing this: if one closes one's eyes and remembers the person, and mentally imposes one's will on the image, it will become symbolic and active.

I have already told you about the *tilak*, and that the science of Yoga has found the third-eye, which is between the two eyebrows, to have great power stored in it – it is a great transmitter. If you ask your son or a servant to do something, and you feel they may refuse, you can do a small experiment. If you concentrate your energy on the center between your eyes and tell them what you want them to do, nine times out of ten they will do it, but if you ask them without concentrating your energy that way, nine times out of ten they will not. Any idea or thought conveyed with the energy concentrated between the two eyes moves rapidly, and carries with it great power.

In the same way, if you concentrate on the image of a person with the energy of the third-eye chakra, and if that thought is then directed at the clay effigy, it no longer remains mere clay. The clay mass becomes energized by your concentrated will. If you mentally infuse some disease into it for one minute, the person whom the clay effigy represents will get that disease. No matter how faraway the person may be from you, he will be affected; he may even die.

Rudolf wrote that what seemed unbelievable actually did happen during his experiments. Before his very eyes he saw tribesmen force a tree, through an earthen replica of it, to dry up and wither. The tree which had been lush, green, and healthy withered, and its leaves became dry. In spite of being watered, within a month the tree became diseased and died. What happened to a tree could happen to a person.

I am talking about these findings of Rudolf's because idol worship is a similar experiment, but on a more profound dimension. If we can transmit disease or death to somebody, there is no reason why we cannot establish or re-establish a relationship with those who are dead. And there is no reason why we should not take a jump by means of an idol into that which is all-pervading and unmanifest.

The whole basis of idol worship is the relationship between your mind and the cosmic mind. What is needed is just a bridge between the two, and that bridge can be made. The idol is an attempt to create that bridge. Only something which is manifest, like the form of an idol, can become the bridge – because it is not possible for you to establish a direct link with the formless.

No matter how much one may talk about the formless and the unmanifest, it is mere talk and does not convey anything to you. Whatever experiences your mind has are all experiences of form and shape; you have no experience of the formless, and words cannot create any resonance in you about that which you have never experienced. You will go on talking about the formless and continue living with form. So if you want to establish a relationship with the formless, you will have to create something which on one side has a form and on the other is formless. That is the secret of the idol.

Let me explain this another way. From our side we need a bridge that has a tangible form, but that also has a formless part: at our end it is manifest, and at the farther end, as it approaches the divine, it becomes unmanifest. If the idol remains just an idol, it cannot act as a bridge; if it is absolutely formless, then it too cannot become a bridge. The idol has to serve two purposes: it has to be visible on our side, and dissolve into the formless on the other.

If I tell you that the term 'idol worship' is wrong, you will be surprised, but actually it is absolutely wrong. It is wrong because for someone who knows how to worship, the idol does not remain just an idol. A person who *only* sees the idol does not know what worship is or how to worship. We are using two words: one is *idol*, and the other is *worship*. These two concepts cannot be experienced by the same person simultaneously. The word *idol* is for those who have never worshipped, and the word *worship* belongs to those who have never seen an idol.

Put differently, we can say that worship is the art of making the idol disappear. It is the art of slowly dropping the manifest and entering the unmanifest. The manifest form gradually dissolves into the unmanifest and as the worship deepens, only the unmanifest remains. So 'idol worship' is self-contradictory. Hence someone who is worshipping will be puzzled as to where the idol is; and someone who has never worshipped will wonder what a stone idol can do. These two types of people have two different types of experiences – and between them there is no common ground.

When you go to a temple, you see only an idol because you are not able to see the worship itself. In a temple, a Meera – the female Indian mystic who is a symbol of devotion – can be found totally absorbed in her worship. For her there is no idol. As soon as real worship deepens, the idol dissolves. We see idols because we do not know what worship is. As less and less worship happens in this world, we will see more and more idols. And once there are many idols, worship will as good as disappear. Furthermore, the idols will have to be destroyed because what use will they be? They will be irrelevant.

Ordinarily, we think that the more primitive a man is, the more likely he is to be an idol-worshipper, and as man becomes more intelligent he drops his idols – but this is not true. In reality, worship has its own science, and the more ignorant we become about it, the more difficult to grasp it seems to us.

In this connection it will be helpful to tell you one more thing. Our belief that man has made progress in all directions, that he has fully evolved, is absolutely wrong. The life of man is so vast, that if he makes great progress in one direction, he does not even realize how far he has remained behind in another direction. If science has made great progress, we have fallen far behind in the matter of religion. Whenever religion flourishes, science lags behind. When we grow in one dimension, the other dimensions are completely forgotten.

In 1880, in Europe, the caves of Altamira were discovered. In those caves there are colored pictures said to have been drawn twenty thousand years ago, but the colors of the pictures look as fresh as if they were painted yesterday. Because of this, Don Marcelino, who discovered these caves, was criticized all over Europe. Everyone thought he had touched up the pictures. All the artists who saw the pictures said Marcelino was trying to fool the public, that such fresh colors could not be ancient.

What they were saying seems right in a way because the paintings of Van Gogh, which are not even one hundred years old, are already fading; the pictures Picasso painted in his youth look as old as he himself. The colors used these days by artists throughout the world do not last more than a hundred years; they are bound to fade within a century.

But when the investigation of the caves Marcelino found was completed, it was proved beyond doubt that the caves were more than twenty thousand years old. This is a great mystery because the people who painted those colors seem to have known much more about colors than we know at present. We have been able to reach the moon, but we have not been able to make colors that can remain fresh and last longer than a hundred years. The people who made these colors twenty thousand years ago knew much more about the science of color than we do.

The mummies of Egypt are five thousand years old. They are the dead bodies of human beings, but because they have been so well preserved, it is as if they had died just yesterday. And we have not been able to discover what preservative mediums might have been used. How could these bodies have been preserved for five thousand years? There is no deterioration at all, but we have not been able to establish which mediums were used to preserve them.

The huge stones on top of the pyramids could not have been placed there by any crane that we have today. It seems beyond the power of man to have put them there, but it is very unlikely the people of that time had cranes. They must have known some technique, which we cannot even guess at, to lift those rocks.

The truths of life are multidimensional. The same work can be done by many different methods and many different techniques. Life is so vast that when we begin to work in one dimension, we forget all other dimensions.

Idols were created by very highly developed people. It is worth thinking about: an idol is a bridge connecting us with the cosmic force which surrounds us, so the people who developed the use of idols created a bridge toward understanding the ultimate mystery of life.

We say that we have discovered electricity. Certainly we are more advanced and sophisticated than earlier communities which knew nothing about electricity. We have discovered radio waves, and we can send a message from one country to another within a second, so we are definitely more advanced than people who depend only on the power of their own voice to communicate just a few hundred feet away, by shouting.

But compared to the people who were able to make a bridge toward contacting the supreme source of life, we are just children. Our electricity, our radio, and similar discoveries are just toys. The art of being connected with the ultimate mystery of life was discovered by people who had worked very hard in that one direction.

As I told you earlier, one aspect of the idol is that which can be seen by man, but a window opens out beyond that form toward the formless. The window of a house must have a shape and a form, just as the house does; the window cannot be formless. But when you open the window and look at the sky, you enter the formless. If I say to someone who has never opened his window to see the sky, 'By opening the window of my house I am able to see the formless,' he will say I am mad. How can one see the infinite from a small window? At the most whatever can be seen from a window can only be as big as the window itself. He is being perfectly logical, and if he has never seen the sky through the window, it will be difficult to convince him that just a small window can open onto the infinite. The window does not set a limitation on that onto which it opens, nor does the idol set a limitation on the formless.

Those who think that an idol is an obstacle in understanding the unmanifest make a great mistake, and those who think that by breaking a window the sky can be broken have helped to create a lot of foolishness in the world. Those who think that by destroying an idol – a form – the formless can be destroyed are no less than mad – but people who do not understand the art and alchemy of worship may well think of destroying idols.

Worship is such an inner, subjective, and personal matter it cannot be expressed or demonstrated. Anything inner and personal in life cannot be demonstrated. If my heart is cut open you will not be able to see love in it; nor will you find anger, hate, forgiveness, or compassion. You will find only a sort of pump for the circulation of blood. If after putting me on the operating table and investigating my heart, a surgeon certifies

I have never experienced any love or hate, I have no way of proving him wrong. Will the surgeon confirm my claim that I have loved? He may say I am deluded, but if I ask the doctor whether *he* has had any experiences of love or hate – and if he is logical and honest – he will say he also has had such delusions. Otherwise, the heart as seen on the operating table is only a pump-like object for the circulation of the blood, and there is nothing like a heart which feels love or hate.

If your eyes are operated on and examined, it will not be possible to prove they have seen dreams. How can you know from an eye opened up on the operating table that at night, while closed, it has seen many dreams? We all see dreams, but where do they exist? Dreams may be unreal, but their existence cannot be denied. However unreal a dream might be, it happened somewhere within. If it was a frightening dream, when you wake up your heart will be beating faster – even if it was unreal; if you cried during your dream, when you wake your eyes will be wet. Something has happened internally, but the outer, the physical eyes, do not reveal anything: whatever is inner, subjective, and personal cannot be seen outwardly.

An idol can be seen – as can the heart or the eye – but worship cannot be seen. Worship is like love or a dream, hence when you pass a temple you can see the idol but not the worship. So if you saw Meera dancing before an idol you would think she was mad, naturally, because her worship cannot be seen – she just seems to be dancing in front of a stone.

When Ramakrishna was appointed to be the priest in the Dakshineshwar temple in Kolkata, after a few days people began to complain about him. It was said that before offering flowers to the deity, Ramakrishna first smelled them himself, before offering the deity food he tasted it himself. This was thought to be sacrilegious.

Ramakrishna was summoned before the temple committee and asked for an explanation. He said that whenever his mother had fed him, she would first test the food to decide whether it was tasty enough for him; she would first decide whether it was worth giving to him – so he was doing the same with the deity. How could he offer food that he had not tasted? How could he offer flowers he had not smelled?

The committee said this went against all the rules of worship, but Ramakrishna asked, 'Can there be any rules for worship? Can there be any rules for love?'

Where there are regulations, worship dies. Where there are regulations, love dies. Love is an outpouring of inner feelings which are very personal and individual. There is a universal truth in this which can be recognized. When two lovers love, though they are both loving, they love in their own individual way. The manifestations may be entirely different, but there is a similarity of experience. Their love may have its own individuality, but within their love the same soul resides.

I was telling you that though the idol can be seen, worship cannot be, but still we have created the expression 'idol worship,' which is absolutely wrong. Worship is the method of obliterating the idol. First the devotee makes the idol and then he makes it disappear. In an earthly sense he makes the idol, and in a spiritual sense he destroys it. He makes it from mud and then lets it dissolve into the ultimate existence.

I will now tell you about one more aspect. In this country for thousands of years we have made idols and then immersed them in water. Many people feel it is a strange thing to do, and they have asked me why beautiful idols are made of the goddess Kali, and then after a few days they are just thrown into the water. Why is the god Ganesha decorated ceremoniously and worshipped lovingly for several days, and then immersed in water, thrown into the sea, a river, or a lake? This is mad! But there is a beautiful concept behind this immersion.

The real secret of worship is in making an idol and then letting it disappear; giving a shape and form to the idol, and then letting it vanish into the formless. It is all symbolic: the act of making an idol of the goddess Kali, worshipping it, and then immersing it in water. But we don't worship in the right way: we make the idol, decorate it beautifully, and look after it, and then we are reluctant to let it go by immersing it. If we had really worshipped, worshipped in the deepest sense, then the idol would have disappeared inside us, been absorbed into us, long before we let it disappear into the water. If real worship had happened, there would have been no need to immerse the idol at all – it might have remained where it was – but the heart of the worshipper would have been immersed into existence, into the divine. Then, if we had gone to immerse the idol, it would have been like throwing away a spent cartridge – it would have done its work.

Nowadays though, when we take the idol to be immersed in the water, it is still like an unspent cartridge – and already we are taking it to be drowned. So naturally we are unhappy about it. In earlier times, during twenty-one days of worship the cartridge would have been fired, it would have already served its purpose; during that time the immersion or disappearance of the idol would have already taken place.

Worship is an immersion. You begin your journey from the idol and proceed through the ritual of worship: as you go ahead, the idol is left behind, and only the state of worship remains. If you stop at the idol you do not know what worship is; if you move into the experience of worship, you will know the root of worship and the real purpose of the idol.

What are the principles involved in the use and worship of an idol? Firstly, in order to jump into the ultimate truth for which you are searching, you need some solid ground, a jumping board. The ultimate truth does not need any solid ground, but *you* need a place from where to set out, from where you can take a jump. You have set out to jump into the ocean, and the ocean is infinite – you will need a shore or coastline from where you can take the jump. Until you jump, where else could you be except on the shore? Once you jump you will have left it behind – but will you not look back to thank the shore from where you jumped into the infinite?

It seems contradictory: how is it possible to jump from form to formlessness? If you are going to be rational about it, then the statement is wrong. How can form lead to the formless? Form should only take you to a deeper form. If you asked Krishnamurti, he would say it is impossible. How can you jump from form to formlessness? How can you jump from the word to the wordless?

But no, all jumps are from form to formlessness because deep down, form is not the opposite of formlessness, but only a part of it – and an indivisible part. It may seem separate to us because of our limited vision, but in fact, form and formlessness are indivisible.

When we are standing on the shore, looking at the ocean, we feel that they are separate; and that this shore and the opposite shore, far across the ocean, are also separate. But if we go deep underneath the water, we will see that this shore and the opposite one are connected at the bottom of the ocean.

If we think in the language of science, there is a very interesting fact: along the bottom of the whole ocean is mud or sand, if we dive into the ocean we will find sand; if we dig into the land, we will find water. Expressed in scientific terms, we could say there is more water and less mud in the ocean, and there is more mud and less water on the land. The difference is only a difference of proportion, of degree, they are not actually separate – everything is one and united.

Whatever we describe as having form is united with the formless; and the formless too is united with form. We are standing in form – and the concept of the idol accepts the fact that we are standing in form. This is the situation, this is where we are; and we can only begin our journey from where we are, not from where we have to reach. Many philosophies begin from where we should ultimately be – but how is it possible to begin a journey from where we are not? The journey has to begin from where we are.

And where are we? We are living in form. All our experiences belong to form, to the manifest. We have not known anything that is not manifest, that does not have a form. If we have loved, we have loved a form; if we have hated, we have hated a form. All our attractions are related to form, and all our repulsions are related to form. Our friends and enemies are all in form; whatsoever we do is done with form.

The original understanding about religious statues and idols accepts this fact; so if we are to set out on our journey to the formless, we will also have to give the formless some form. Of course, that form will be according to our own likings.

One person experiences the formless in Mahavira, someone else in Krishna, and still another in Jesus. Whosoever has seen the formless in Jesus, by looking into his eyes, has found a door which opens into the formless sky; and whosoever has held Jesus' hand has found that it ceased to be his hand, it has become the hand of the infinite. If someone who has heard Jesus' words and felt his heart vibrate – not in response to the words, but to what was beyond those words – has created a statue of Jesus and worshipped it, there can be no easier way than this to make the jump into the formless.

Someone has found the formless in Krishna, someone has found it in Buddha, and someone else has found it in Mahavira. But remember: at first we will only be able to see the formless, the infinite, through some form; pure formlessness cannot be seen directly by anyone. We don't have the capacity to see it directly – the formless has to come to us bound in a form.

This is what a divine incarnation means – that the formless has assumed a shape and a form, that the infinite has chosen to show you a tangible, bodily form. It seems self-contradictory, but this is what a divine incarnation is. A divine incarnation is a sort of platform from where you can see the vast sky. A divine incarnation is a glimpse of the formless. You cannot have a direct contact with the formless – the experience of it will be through some form. And once this happens, the experience can be repeated through that form again and again very easily.

Whosoever has seen Buddha will find him rising, alive, from his picture or image. For whoever loves Buddha, his statue will slowly disappear and Buddha's living being will be felt there. Buddha, Mahavira, Krishna, or Christ – all of them leave behind devices through which to contact them. Through these devices their devotees can establish contact with them; so the form of the statue is a very specific arrangement.

The art and science of making a religious statue consists of many concepts and calculations. If these are remembered while making the statue, then that statue can lead you deeper into meditation. In this connection it will be good to remember two or three things.

If you have seen any of Buddha's statues, you will have observed that they represent a certain state of being rather than a particular individual. If you look deeply at a statue of Buddha, within a few moments you will feel that great compassion is showering on you from all around. Buddha's raised hand, his half-closed eyes, his proportionately sculptured face, his graceful expression, his delicate way of sitting – all are in some deeper sense meant to evoke compassion in you.

When someone asked the great French artist Cézanne why he painted, he said, 'I draw pictures only to find what form a certain emotion, a certain feeling of my heart, will take on a canvas. In my efforts to express that feeling, a picture emerges.'

If someone meditates on that picture, he can experience the same emotion that was present in the painter's heart.

When you look at a painting you see just the form, you are not aware of such a phenomenon – but then you will also not be able to understand the soul of the painter. If someone were to draw some crisscross lines on a canvas, they would not just be crisscross. If you concentrate on them, something will go crisscross within you too – because it is the nature of the mind that it vibrates in you with a similar resonance to that which it sees outside itself. If the same lines were drawn with a particular symmetry, looking at them your mind too would attain to some harmony.

You probably do not know that the joy you feel when you look at a flower is not so much because of the flower itself, but because of the symmetry of its petals, which is also induced in you. When you are attracted to the beauty in someone's face, it is not because of that person's beauty, but because it corresponds to your inner image of beauty. It produces a resonance of beauty in you, which makes you feel that something within you is also beautified. In a similar way, the presence of an ugly face makes something within you feel uncomfortable. The experience of joy in the presence of someone who is beautiful is because of the flow of beauty which it brings about in you, making you also more beautiful. Ugliness means that something is without proportion, gross, asymmetrical, and unbalanced; and this evokes in us a feeling of disharmony, repulsion, disorder and discomfort.

When Nijinsky committed suicide, people went to his house to investigate the situation, and came out within ten or fifteen minutes feeling a sense of uneasiness. They said it did not feel good to go into his house, and that anyone who stayed in it for as long as Nijinsky had would also commit suicide. What was it about his house which was so unpleasant? He had painted all the walls and ceilings red and black – for two years it had been like this. It was not surprising that he went mad and committed suicide. The people who went inside his house said anyone staying in that house for two years would also have gone mad, and not to have committed suicide for two years showed that Nijinsky must have been a very courageous man! The whole atmosphere of the house was utterly chaotic.

Whatsoever you see creates its echo within you; in some deep sense you become like that which you see. All statues of Buddha are made to reflect compassion because that is his inner message. Buddha said if you have compassion you have everything. But what does compassion mean? It does not mean love. Love comes and goes but compassion is a love which, once it comes, never goes. In love, there is a subtle desire to get something from the other. In compassion, there is the awareness that no one has anything to give; everyone is so poor that there is nothing they can give, and that is why there is compassion. There is no demand in compassion. In this state there is no desire even to give, but the effect of such compassion is that all the doors of the heart become wide open and something spontaneously begins to be distributed.

Buddha told his disciples, 'When you meditate, worship, or pray, remember to immediately distribute whatsoever peace you receive. Don't keep it with you even for a moment – I call you irreligious if you do so. When you are full of joy after meditation, immediately pray to the supreme being to let that joy be distributed to those who need it. Open the doors of your heart and let the joy flow toward all those who need it – just as water flows down the mountains.'

This great compassion is described by Buddha as the ultimate liberation. So, all the statues of Buddha were made in such a way that, in their presence, the worshipper would feel the resonance and vibrations of compassion within himself.

But how can you worship a statue of Buddha? I am taking this one example to make things more clear to you. If you want to worship a statue of Buddha, the center of worship will be the heart. If you don't know this, you will never be able to understand Buddha's statue because the very purpose of it is to create compassion in you. The center of compassion is the heart, so while worshipping Buddha, our awareness on the one side should be on his heart, and on the other side on our own heart. You will have to dive deeply into the feeling where both hearts are beating in one rhythm. A moment will come when you feel a thread connecting your heart to that within Buddha's statue. You will not only feel it, but you will be able to see the pulsation of the statue's heart with open eyes. When that happens, you will know that life has been imparted to the statue; otherwise there is no life in it, and worshipping it is meaningless.

The heart of the statue can be seen to be pulsating, if you have rightly meditated on the pulsations of your heart, and at the same time on Buddha's heart, a relationship will be established between the two. Then your heart will be beating with Buddha's, just as you see your face reflected in a mirror.

Have you ever watched your heart beating in a mirror? You will say a mirror is a mirror, it is bound to reflect all movements. In a deep sense, in a deeper religious sense, an idol can also be a mirror. So your heart and that of the idol will pulsate. Until this happens, worship cannot begin because the idol is still only of stone; life has not been invoked into it.

If you want to meditate on the statue of Buddha, the center has to be the heart. If you want to meditate on Mahavira, there is a different center, for Jesus there is another center, and for Krishna yet another. All statues are made with a different center as the basis. Even though a society may have been worshipping a certain idol for thousands of years, it may not be aware of its center, and if the center is not known, you cannot establish a connection with the statue. You may offer flowers and incense, you may bow down to it, but you will have done it all before a mere stone. Remember, the stone has to be transformed into a deity! That part will not be done by the sculptor, it will have to be done by you. The sculptor will only give it a shape. Who will pour life into it? Life has to be instilled into it by the devotee. Without that, it is just a stone. Worship begins only after life has been given to the statue.

And what is worship? Once you are able to invoke life in a statue, you are worshipping a real, alive deity. Try to understand this deeply: as soon as something becomes alive, the form and the formless are both present in it – the body is the form, and the life that is in it is the formless. Life has no form.

If someone cuts off my hand, my life is not cut off. If I was hypnotized or anesthetized and my hand was cut off, I would not feel any pain. My whole brain can be removed without my becoming aware that it is no longer inside the body – because life as such has no shape or form. Wherever there is life, there is a meeting of form and formlessness.

Matter has form, consciousness has none. As long as an idol is just a stone, there is only shape and form, but as soon as a devotee invokes life into it, it becomes alive. Remember, the worshipper who cannot bring his heart to pulsate in the statue will not be able to have the heart of the ultimate pulsate within himself. This is the very criterion. As soon as the devotee is able to make his heart pulsate within the idol, the idol is brought to life: and then, simultaneously, at one end it has form, and at the other end it becomes the door to the formless. To travel through this door is worship. Worship is the journey from form to formlessness.

There are several steps to worship, but the first and fundamental one is to understand that every individual is self-centered. Our whole way of living is as though 'I am' is the center of the whole world: 'The moon and the stars rise for me, the birds are flying for my joy, and the sun too is giving light for me: the whole world is revolving around me, I am the center of the whole world.' Such a person cannot know worship, feeling that he is at the center and the rest of the world is his circumference.

In worship you see the opposite: the fundamental law of worship is, 'I am on the circumference, the center is somewhere else.'

An irreligious man's basic philosophy is that he is the center and the rest of the world is the periphery. Even if God exists, he is on the periphery: 'He is there for me. If I am sick, he must cure me. If my son is unemployed, he must get him a job. If I'm in trouble, God has to run to my aid.'

This type of theism is worse than atheism. Such a person does not understand what he is saying.

The right meaning of worship, the right meaning of prayer, of being religious, is to understand that you are on the periphery and existence is the center. As soon as the heart of the image is alive and pulsating, as soon as one experiences that the image is alive, formlessness has entered it. So the basic foundation for worship is the feeling: 'I am on the periphery. I will dance for you, sing for you, live for you, and breathe for you – and whatever happens will be for you, the center.'

A great sage named Totapuri was once staying with Ramakrishna. He asked Ramakrishna how long he was going to remain obsessed with an idol – it was time he began his journey into the formless. Ramakrishna replied that he was ready to start his journey. In fact, Ramakrishna was always ready to learn anything from anybody; he was always ready to learn from whosoever wanted to teach, but he asked Totapuri to wait until he got permission from his mother.

'Which mother?' Totapuri asked.

Ramakrishna replied, 'My mother, the goddess Kali.'

Totapuri said, 'But that's exactly what I am talking about! How long will you go on being caught up with that stone idol of Kali? Do you want to ask that stone?'

Ramakrishna replied, 'There is no other way but to ask her. From the moment I began to worship her, she became the center and I moved to the circumference. Now that I am not, she has to be asked permission. Whatever I do is for her; without her permission even enlightenment is meaningless. If she orders me to go to hell, I am ready; but without asking her, nothing can be done.'

Totapuri could not understand this. If Ramakrishna had to ask Kali permission to stop worshipping her, how would she grant it? Do we ask the permission of a person we want to drop? Is permission needed to drop something?

By this time Ramakrishna had gone to the temple. Totapuri followed him. He saw tears coming from Ramakrishna's eyes: he was begging Kali again and again to allow him to stop worshipping her. He told her that Totapuri was waiting for him. Then suddenly he became joyous and began dancing. Totapuri, who was standing behind him, asked what had happened.

Ramakrishna said, 'She has given her permission! Now I am ready to learn from you!'

The meaning of having someone as your center is that your life is now a surrendered life. Worshipping implies a surrendered life. Worshipping the divine means living as the divine wishes: sitting and standing, eating and drinking, speaking and remaining silent, too, for the divine.

As soon as the formless becomes one's center, a mysterious current begins to flow, a sort of expansion begins. As it is, we have contracted ourselves, but when the seed cracks open, it begins to become a tree. We have contracted ourselves in our 'I', but when that 'I' cracks open, sprouts come out and the expansion begins. These sprouts can expand enough to encompass the whole world.

Religion is full of many surprises, but we don't understand how such a thing might happen because from our very birth we have believed ourselves to be the center of the world.

Buddha used to suggest that his disciples spend some time in a cremation ground. They needed to be there for three months before they could be initiated as monks. They would say they had come to learn from him, not from the cremation grounds, but Buddha would insist and say, 'After three months in the burning grounds, your "I" will be surrendered and it will be easier to teach you. For three months every day, you will see bodies being burned and at least once during the three months, you will begin to think this world does not exist for you alone. When you were not here, the world existed. This person whose body you are watching being burned also thought just moments before his death that the world existed for him. The world does not even know now that this person is no more. The ocean does not notice that a wave has vanished.

'So go on watching, and when you realize that the world does not exist for you, come to me – then real meditation can begin. As long as you are at the center there is no possibility of real worship, of prayer or meditation; there is only a deep illusion. Worship will begin when that illusion vanishes; worship begins when 'I' is dropped and 'thou' becomes significant.'

Remember: first the devotee makes the statue disappear and opens the door to the formless. Then he makes himself disappear and worship begins. As soon as a door to the formless opens through a statue, the dissolution of one's ego becomes easier. As soon as the devotee realizes that a stone idol can disappear to become a door to the formless, he realizes that he too can become a door to the formless, that if he can forget his so-called self, a deeper jump becomes possible.

There can be a distinction between two forms, but this does not apply as far as the formless is concerned because the formless is only one. When the statue has become formless and the devotee has become formless, then there is nothing like 'two'. Numbers have no value in relation to the formless.

This is the basis, but there are many methods and techniques to make use of this basis. In this connection there are a few things to be understood.

Sufis have given great importance to dancing as worship. Devotees like Meera and Chaitanya also attached great value to dancing – it has a few qualities which have led to many devotional disciplines choosing it as a method.

The first effect of dancing is that while dancing, more than at any other time, you experience that you are not the body – because of the fast movements of the dance, you feel that you and your body are separate. In reality there is a relationship between your body and your consciousness; it is a well-arranged relationship, and in your day-to-day work that relationship is never broken.

Gurdjieff used to say that if there are many pebbles in a container, and you shake the container vigorously, the arrangement of things inside will be disturbed. A pebble that was lying at the bottom will come to the top, one lying in the middle will move to the side, and one which was on top will be in the middle; the whole arrangement within the can will become topsy-turvy. If a pebble was used to being in a certain place in relation to the other pebbles, and if it had become identified with that position, its ego would be destroyed. The stone would feel, 'I am no more,' it was only part of an arrangement and that arrangement no longer existed.

So Meera, Chaitanya, and the Sufis have made profound use of dancing. Dervish dancing goes very deep. In it, the dancer's body spins so fast and with such a totality that every cell and fiber of his body vibrates. This breaks the relationship between the body and the consciousness, and suddenly the dancer realizes that he is separate from his body. So using dance for worship is very valuable.

There are two Christian sects, one of which is known as the Quakers and the other as the Shakers – the Quakers, even today, are quite influential. The names of these sects are very descriptive: during their worship, the Shakers shake the body for hours, so vigorously that the whole body – its every cell – becomes a trembling, and the Shaker perspires heavily. At that point, where the body is shaking strongly, he will experience that his consciousness is separate from the body, and then that consciousness moves into prayer.

The Quakers' name too is meaningful: their bodies can quake very strongly when they worship. Just as in an earthquake the ground shakes so much that everything comes crashing down, Quakers get into such a quaking that the body's connection with its consciousness is broken. All of these types of movement, dance, and devotional song have been used to create a gap between the body and consciousness.

In this connection, let us understand a little about the science of sound. Science believes that the ultimate unit of all matter is electricity. Eastern sages believe the ultimate unit of matter is not electricity, but sound. Modern physics believes that ultimately all matter is made up of electricity, whereas Eastern sages say sound is the basic unit of all matter. Whatever the truth may be, the thing to be understood is that there is a close relationship between electricity and sound. It is possible the statements of the scientist and the sage are both true, simultaneously.

If not today, then tomorrow, the reality of the ultimate element will be known: one form of that element is sound, and the other is electricity – what that element is has yet to be discovered. Searching from the religious aspect, the sage reaches the knowledge that sound is the ultimate; searching from the material aspect, the scientist has been led to electricity. Remember, the sage has searched within himself, not within matter: within your self, the ultimate experience of your existence is that of sound. As long as you are aware of yourself, there will be the awareness of sound. The deeper you go within yourself, the less audible the sound will be, until it becomes a void. That very silence has its own sound, the 'soundless sound,' which Indian sages have described as *anahat nada*, unstruck sound. That unstruck sound is the ultimate sound; the last experience of human consciousness before it enters the formless is this sound. Because of this experience, Indian sages say that sound is the ultimate element.

The scientist divides and subdivides matter into its smallest component, and just before it disappears into the formless it is seen as the electron. Then, when matter is completely lost and formlessness happens, for him what remains is electricity.

What has to be considered is whether the smallest, the ultimate, part of consciousness exists even before the smallest part of matter. It is certain that consciousness is more subtle than matter, hence the ultimate part of consciousness must exist before that of matter. That is why Indian sages have held the view that sound is more subtle than electricity, that it precedes electricity and is the ultimate source of everything.

Music, prayer, and mantra chanting are all uses of sound. Every sound creates a particular state within you; there is no sound which does not. Scientists who are experimenting with sound electronics now know that if particular musical instruments are played in front of a plant, it will grow flowers a month earlier than it would have otherwise. If particular musical instruments are played in front of cows, they will give more milk, but if the wrong instruments are used, or the wrong music is played, they may not give any milk at all.

Sound reaches within you and strikes your consciousness. A sword may cut your neck, but with the 'sword of sound' your mind can be cut. The blade of sound is sharper and disconnects your mind from its various preoccupations. So experiments have been done with the blade of sound, in which sound is used to cut off the mind of a meditator or a devotee, so he can begin his journey to the infinite. All religions have used special sounds and refined them through thousands of years of experimentation.

Recently someone from Japan came to me. For the last two years he has been doing an exercise from the Soto School of Zen. In this exercise he makes the sound of Mu, mu most of his waking time. This sound is uttered continuously except when he rests and eats. He gets up at three in the morning, takes a bath, and begins to repeat Mu, mu. He does this for three days, and his thoughts become less and less. The sound of Mu, mu continues to reverberate; a sort of storm is created within. It becomes like a sword and cuts off all thinking.

After seven days he does not need to create the sound: it continues on its own, and spreads all over his body. Whatsoever he may be doing – sitting or walking, anything – within him the silent repetition of Mu, mu continues. Every cell and every fiber vibrates with its rhythm. It is difficult to eat, because the sound of Mu is going on. After seven days, sleep is difficult too because his mouth goes on repeating Mu, mu. During whatever sleep he does have, the sound goes deeper and deeper.

After twenty-one days, he begins to shout and roar the sound Mu, mu like a lion. His eyes, his face, and his behavior change. His teacher goes on pushing him to continue. Once he begins to roar, his eating, drinking and sleeping drop. In the fourth week he becomes as if mad – a state where he has no awareness of anything except the sound Mu, mu. If you ask his name, he will reply, Mu. He loses all awareness of his body, only the awareness of Mu remains. He does not know who he is. At this stage he has to be watched over and guarded – he may do anything, he may go anywhere.

In the last stage, he roars with his total strength. It is as if some wound has opened or a ghost has possessed him. And then everything calms down – a huge wave of the ocean has taken its last leap and fallen apart. The climax has passed and everything within him has scattered.

He falls down and remains without moving, quiet and peaceful, for one to three weeks. When he comes back he is not the same person – he is a new man. The old man has died: now nothing that was old – his anger, his desires, his greed – can be traced. The continuity with his past is broken. With this experiment of Mu, with this great explosion of sound, his whole consciousness is transformed.

'Om' is a similar sound. All religions have their own sounds which are used in worship. As the worship deepens, the impact of these sounds transforms the devotee. Devotional singing and the playing of musical instruments are also sound impacts, and that is why repetition is significant. If you sing one song today, a different one tomorrow and a third on the next day, there will be no result. There must be a continuous hammering on the same particular center.

If you hammer a tent peg into different spots, it will never go into the ground. If you dig two feet at one place, two feet at another place, and two feet at yet another, you will never be able to dig a well. Similarly, changing centers, like places, does not bring results. To dig a well, digging has to be done in one spot only.

That is why repetition has been insisted upon – so much so that for a whole month you have to repeat Mu or 'Om' or a single line of a song, again and again, in the same rhythm. But there is a danger that the repetition becomes mechanical, as if it is just a job to be done, and then it will be useless.

The repetition has to be a question of life and death, as if you are totally staking everything on it. Every hair, every cell, every fiber of the body participates; every nerve, every bone, every piece of flesh and muscle becomes involved; every drop of blood has to call aloud. When your whole existence becomes that sound, there will be results. The devotee has to repeat only one word, or a line of a song, for years together, for a particular reason: to hammer on one spot again and again so that perhaps the door breaks open – and it does.

So sound, dancing, singing, and music have all been used in worship. They have all been done in front of an idol – this should be remembered because dancing as such is a different matter. Many people dance, but they do not become enlightened. If they are dancing for the sake of dancing, then this has no relationship with enlightenment. So everything has to be done in relationship to the formless, the infinite – and hence in front of the idol that has been made alive by your devotion. The idol will continuously remind you that the dance is not for the sake of dancing. The dancing is on the periphery: the center is the idol, the center is in the supreme being. All is in preparation for a jump into the ultimate. Otherwise, there are dancers, musicians, and singers who are all superb in their art – better than any devotee – but this is not the point; the devotee is not concerned with music or song, his purpose is different. His whole effort is to become so overwhelmed that he can dissolve and lose himself so fully that the inner flow takes over and sets him afloat in the infinite. He has to become the circumference, with the ultimate at the center; he has to create such liquidness that he can remain afloat and flow.

You will often find a devotee with tears flowing down his cheeks. He is not weeping out of unhappiness, but out of joy. Tears flow only when something within has become liquid, fluid – either out of misery or overwhelming joy.

Up to now, scientists have not been able to explain the purpose of tears: at best, they have discovered that tears are meant for cleaning the eyes of dust. Tear glands are only meant to clean the eyes, but why do tears flow when one is in pain, when one is unhappy, or when one is overjoyed? Does dust only fall into the eyes at those particular times, and not otherwise?

Whenever there is an overflowing, whenever there is an extreme of pain or pleasure, tears begin to flow. The tear glands open and tears flow out. Devotees also weep, but their weeping has a different quality. Someone who is not a devotee will not be able to understand it. What happens to a devotee that makes him weep? You may think he must have some difficulties, and that he is weeping with folded hands because of this, but someone who is weeping because of his difficulties still has himself as the center. He is still not a devotee – he does not know what worship is.

But there are moments when all the frozenness and rigidity which has solidified within us begins to liquefy, and the awareness of that happening makes tears flow. These tears flow in gratitude and thankfulness toward existence. We have nothing but our tears to give to the grace that is flowing toward us. We feel we do not deserve whatever we are receiving, and that we cannot contain the joy that is descending on us. We had never even dreamed of such a feeling, and we have no way to show our gratitude. Neither words nor anything else can adequately express it.

In such moments, the eyes weep in a different way. The devotee's eyes weep differently from those of a lover. The lover weeps, but that weeping has a different quality. The lover's tears are full of small desires and demands, but there are no demands in the devotee's tears. His eyes weep for no reason; he is simply helpless. Even when he wants to express his gratitude, words do not come out of his mouth, and when the mouth cannot speak, the eyes begin to speak in their own way. The perfection, the completion of worship, is in tears, in their fluidity and in their flowing.

Religious statues have been used in many different ways to experience ecstasy. Those who speak against such things do not know what worship means. Anything can be said by someone who does not know; what is said by an ignorant person is not of much value. In this century, this kind of teaching has taken root because others also do not know. When nobody knows what is what, there is no choice but to believe whatever is said.

If someone says 'There is no God,' he does not have to prove anything, but whosoever says 'There is a God' has to prove it. So the mind easily goes with that which is negative, but hesitates to go with anything positive because it will have to take the trouble to prove it. Worship is positive, religious statues are positive. And in denying something, there is nothing to lose.

Turgenev has written a small story . . .

In a certain town there was a very intelligent man, a genius. And in the same town there lived an utter fool, an idiot. One day the idiot approached the intelligent man and asked to be shown a way of becoming intelligent. The intelligent man asked the idiot whether he wanted to *be* intelligent or *appear to be* intelligent because to become intelligent was a long process, but to look intelligent was easy. The idiot replied he wanted to be shown the easier way. It was enough if he looked intelligent – he did not want to bother about becoming intelligent.

The intelligent man commented that in becoming intelligent there was a possibility of making a mistake, but in looking intelligent there could be no mistake. The idiot became impatient and requested that the trick be revealed without any delay. So the intelligent man whispered something in his ear and from that day on, the idiot gradually began to become known as intelligent throughout the town.

The people of the town began to gossip: How had this fool suddenly become intelligent? What had the intelligent man told him?

He had simply told the fool to immediately negate every statement he heard. If anyone said, 'There is something to idol worship,' the idiot was immediately to reply there was not. The idiot asked the intelligent man, 'Should I say such things even when I don't know anything about the subject?'

The intelligent man said, 'You don't have to bother about knowing anything at all – just negate whatever is said. If anyone tells you the works of Kalidas are wonderful, just say it is all rubbish. Ask them to prove that they are wonderful! If anyone says that some music is heavenly, say such music is played even in hell, and ask the person to prove what heavenly music is like. Just deny everything, and if anyone opposes you, challenge him to prove his claim.'

Within two weeks, the idiot became famous for his intelligence throughout the town. People started saying that he was very deep, and difficult to judge or understand. If someone said Tagore's poetry is beautiful, he replied that it is simply rubbish – any schoolchild could write such poems.

Then the person felt shaky because it was difficult to prove what he was saying.

This century is, in a way, a century of many types of foolishnesses. And the foundation of our foolishness is negation. For a whole century we have been denying one thing after another. When others are not able to prove something, they also join in the negating – but remember the more negative a life is, the more insignificant it becomes.

No truth can be known without being positive. The more negative a life is, although outwardly it will seem more intelligent, inwardly it will be more stupid. The more negative a life is, the less it will be possible for truth, bliss, and beauty to penetrate it because all elevating experiences happen only to a positive mind. All experiences of value happen only to a positive mind.

Whenever someone says no, something within his mind closes. Have you ever thought about the effect of words? If you close yourself in your room and loudly say no, you will find that your whole heart contracts and becomes closed. If you say yes loudly, you will find that your heart opens its wings and flies into the sky. Words are not just born; the uttering of them creates some parallel event. In saying no, something contracts within you, and in saying yes, something opens within you.

Someone asked Saint Augustine, 'What is your worship? What is your prayer?'

Saint Augustine replied, 'Yes, yes and yes, my Lord! This is my worship, this is my whole prayer.'

The man may not have understood what Saint Augustine had said, but whoever says yes to his life in its totality is a theist. Theism does not mean just saying yes to the existence of God; it is the capacity to say yes. The atheist does not just deny the existence of God, the atheist has no other capacity except to say no. Such a person will go on shrinking and contracting, and will ultimately decay, but saying yes makes a person open up, and expand so much that he merges with the infinite.

Worshipping an idol or a statue is a very positive method, but you have to meditate and go so deep into the idol, into the worship, that you come to know there is no idol, there is only worship – the idol is just the beginning.

It is true that the worship too is of nothing less than the divine, yet in an even deeper sense, you will find that it is your own transformation. The divine is just an excuse, and that excuse makes it easy to transform oneself.

Doctor Rudolf, about whom I was speaking earlier, developed an important principle that will be useful for you to know about. Whenever a thought arises in your mind, it has to travel through the nerves and muscles and through the whole mechanism of the body. For example, if the thought arises in my mind to love you and to take your hand in mine, immediately this thought begins to travel – passing from the brain through the mechanism of the body, until it reaches my fingertips.

Rudolf says that when a thought is born it has the power of one hundred units; by the time it reaches the fingertips, only one unit remains. Ninety-nine units of power are used up in the transmission, in translating that thought into action. All thoughts become lifeless by the time they reach the outer surface of the body – that is why more happiness is actually experienced at the thought of taking your beloved's hand than the experience of it. At the moment of the experience you feel that the experience is not as satisfying as you had expected. What happened? Why was the fulfillment of the thought less fulfilling than the thought itself?

When someone thinks about making love he feels elated, but after making love he is left feeling depressed. He feels it was not so great after all. Why? When the thought was conceived it had the potentiality of a hundred units, but by the time it reached the periphery it was reduced to one unit. Sometimes the potentiality becomes zero or even negative: if the body is sick or weak, so much energy is dissipated while it is traveling to the periphery that it can even become negative. So if you are sick, you may have expected to feel happy when you held your beloved's hand, but instead, by the time the thought has traveled to your hand, taking her hand makes you unhappy. The experience becomes negative. Rudolf says that if this is true, then man will never become happy.

Is there a way that one's thought can directly jump into another's mind? – religion says there is. And through hundreds of experiments, Rudolf has also confirmed that my thought can take a direct jump into another's mind, without using the medium of my physical body. To do so, I stop my thought at the third-eye center by closing my eyes, and make it jump directly to your third eye. The whole system of telepathy depends on this art.

Rudolf demonstrated this by transmitting a thought one thousand miles; other experiments, at Harvard, in Russia and in many other countries, have given proof of telepathy. In this experiment you concentrate your thought on your third eye, as if your thought has become a small sun revolving rapidly in your mind; that small sun becomes focused and highly potent. The thought is not allowed to spread to the rest of the body – which would allow loss of energy. The energy has to accumulate at one point where it remains focused like a strong ray of light. Just when you feel that it cannot become more focused, more concentrated: that is the moment for the thought to jump. At exactly that moment, you have to project the thought into the mind of the other person. However faraway the person may be, he must be in your field of imagination, and you need to imagine that the thought has entered the mind of the other person through his third eye. Once this happens, the thought is transferred.

Telepathy is the art of projecting a thought into someone else without any physical medium. The third eye has been meditated on in many ways for religious purposes. It can be used for communicating with the cosmic mind as well as with the human mind. For example, you are sitting in front of Mahavira's statue: Mahavira's consciousness has become one with the infinite, but if you concentrate your total energy at the third-eye center and project it into the statue's head, your thought will be transmitted to the consciousness of Mahavira. In this way, many people who have come after Mahavira have been helped. For such people, Buddha, Mahavira, and Christ are not dead, but alive here and now. For them there is a direct communion.

This experiment can also be used to take a direct jump into the infinite. But how will you find the third eye of the infinite? To where will you project your thought energy? To where will you transmit it?

It will be easier to communicate through the medium of an idol; directly projecting the thought beam into the infinite is difficult. It can be done, but for that there is a different technique; the religions which have not used idols or statues of religious figures have used that technique, but it is very difficult. So even those religions which did not at first use idols finally came around to using them.

Islam has not used idols, but the mosque has become the idol; and the graves of Mohammedan saints are worshipped. Even today, in any part of the world, when a Mohammedan says his prayers, he faces the direction of the Kaaba. Those who know about it have used the Kaaba as a medium through which to transmit their third-eye thoughts. Those who do not understand the secret meaning just stand facing the direction of the Kaaba while they pray.

It does not make any difference whether you project onto the Kaaba or an idol; it makes no difference whether you kiss the feet of the idol or the stone of Kaaba – it is one and the same. There is no photograph of Mohammed, there is no statue of Mohammed, but what difference has it made? Something else was done. No statue or picture of Mohammed was ever made, but devotees shower flowers on the tombs of Moslem saints. It was not possible to find an equally powerful substitute for Mohammed.

So if Krishna instructs his devotees to bow down at the feet of his image, he is farsighted in understanding their problems; Krishna knew that it is very difficult for a man to avoid using an idol. Taking a direct jump into the infinite is so difficult only one in ten people might succeed – then what will happen to the rest? If Krishna's statue is not available, they will just use any idol, which will be very ordinary.

What has been the effect of prohibiting the use of an idol of Mohammed? If a Mohammedan fakir dies in some town, Mohammedans gather around his tomb. The Mohammedans are not wrong in doing this; it is the inner nature of man that is responsible. To me, what a statue of Mohammed could have done cannot be done by the tomb of a fakir. Although Mohammed was right in saying there is no need for a statue, this is true for only one man in a million. And such a person needs nothing to reach anyway: he does not need an idol, a Kaaba, a Koran, or the Gita; he also does not need Mohammed, Krishna, or Buddha. For him, everything is unnecessary, he can attain directly – but what about others?

For the rest, all those things are needed, and when something is needed, it is better to have the best. It is better, instead of worshipping the tomb of a fakir or the statue of some virtuous villager, to have the statue of a Buddha, a Krishna, or a Mahavira. When you have to travel by sea, it is risky to go by a small, locally-made boat – it is better to travel in an ocean liner. When Buddha's ship is available, it is stupid to depend on an amulet made by some fakir, or on the grave of a person whose blessings may have helped some people to recover from a disease. But if Buddha's statue is not available, because of man's inner need he will look for a substitute.

Superficially it seems as if those who have rejected the worship of idols and statues have said something great, but those who are in favor of idol worship have the experience of thousands of years, and they know from experience that a person will need an idol. Most people have a limitation in that they cannot reach the formless directly, they need a rest stop on the way – and the more beautiful and comfortable the place is the better.

There has been no society on earth which did not worship some kind of idol. No group of human beings has existed in any corner of the earth which did not use an idol in one form or other. This indicates that the idol fulfills some inherent need, not just for the individual, but for the whole of humanity. It is only in this century, or the last two hundred years, that the concept of the idol has been shattered. Some people argue that idols are a meaningless burden, just stones, and they must be removed, but if the meaning behind such worship were first properly understood, I don't think an intelligent person would want to remove the idols. If the scientific thinking behind idol worship is not understood, then the idols will have to be removed; they cannot be saved, and they will probably fall away by themselves.

Today people worship idols and statues without understanding, and bow down before them without knowing why. Their hearts do not participate – it is just a formality that has remained. Such people will only be the cause of the destruction of the idol because although they worship every day, there is no transformation in their lives, and hence it seems futile to worship an idol or a statue.

A person worships an idol for forty years, and nothing happens to him. Then he drags his son to the temple too. When the son asks his father, if he has not got anything out of forty years of worship, why is he being forced to go to the temple, there is no answer. If something had happened in the father, the question would not have arisen.

There is a small fable by Aesop . . .

In a forest, a lion was asking every animal he came across whether he was the king of the forest or not. He asked a bear, and the bear said, 'You are definitely king.'

Then he asked a leopard, who hesitated a little, but then said, yes, the lion is the king.

Then the lion asked the elephant, who immediately picked him up in his trunk and threw him a great distance. While he was in mid air, the lion said to the elephant, 'O great being, if you didn't know the answer, you could have simply said so. You didn't need to throw me away – I would have gone of my own accord!'

But the elephant that is powerful enough to lift up and throw the lion does not need to make any reply. It is not necessary for him to say who the king is.

Someone who worships an idol would not need to reply if he truly knew what worship was. His life would be the answer. His eyes, the way he sits and stands would become the reply. But those who do not know what worship is and still go on worshipping are responsible for the declining interest in idols.

They do not know what real worship is, but the idols have remained in their hands.

It is because of this that I have talked to you about worship – so you might understand that an idol is a method meant for total, inner transformation. The idol is just an excuse.

It is like hanging your coat on a peg. The purpose of the peg is just to hang the coat on. If there were no peg, the coat would have been hung up on the door, on a chair; it has to be hung somewhere. But once it is hung up, you cannot see the peg, and so you don't ask any questions about it.

The idol is just a peg – worship is the actual purpose.

But while worshipping the idol you don't see the worship – you don't see the coat, you only see the peg. You feel the peg has spoiled the wall – why keep it?

You don't know anything about worship. Only the idol remains, utterly helpless and defeated. It may not survive – it is only the life force of worship that can save it. That is why I have talked to you about worship.

About Osho

Osho's unique contribution to the understanding of who we are defies categorization. Mystic and scientist, a rebellious spirit whose sole interest is to alert humanity to the urgent need to discover a new way of living. To continue as before is to invite threats to our very survival on this unique and beautiful planet.

His essential point is that only by changing ourselves, one individual at a time, can the outcome of all our 'selves' – our societies, our cultures, our beliefs, our world – also change. The doorway to that change is meditation.

Osho the scientist has experimented and scrutinized all the approaches of the past and examined their effects on the modern human being and responded to their shortcomings by creating a new starting point for the hyperactive 21st Century mind: OSHO Active Meditations.

Once the agitation of a modern lifetime has started to settle, 'activity' can melt into 'passivity,' a key starting point of real meditation. To support this next step, Osho has transformed the ancient 'art of listening' into a subtle contemporary methodology: the OSHO Talks. Here words become music, the listener discovers who is listening, and the awareness moves from what is being heard to the individual doing the listening. Magically, as silence arises, what needs to be heard is understood directly, free from the distraction of a mind that can only interrupt and interfere with this delicate process.

These thousands of talks cover everything from the individual quest for meaning to the most urgent social and political issues facing society today. Osho's books are not written but are transcribed from audio and video recordings of these extemporaneous talks to international audiences. As he puts it, 'So remember: whatever I am saying is not just for you...I am talking also for the future generations.'

Osho has been described by *Sunday Times* in London as one of the '1000 Makers of the 20th Century' and by American author Tom Robbins as 'the most dangerous man since Jesus Christ.' *Sunday Mid-Day* (India) has selected Osho as one of ten people – along with Gandhi, Nehru and Buddha – who have changed the destiny of India.

About his own work Osho has said that he is helping to create the conditions for the birth of a new kind of human being. He often characterizes this new human being as 'Zorba the Buddha' – capable both of enjoying the earthy pleasures of a Zorba the Greek and the silent serenity of a Gautama the Buddha.

Running like a thread through all aspects of Osho's talks and meditations is a vision that encompasses both the timeless wisdom of all ages past and the highest potential of today's (and tomorrow's) science and technology.

Osho is known for his revolutionary contribution to the science of inner transformation, with an approach to meditation that acknowledges the accelerated pace of contemporary life. His unique OSHO Active Meditations™ are designed to first release the accumulated stresses of body and mind, so that it is then easier to take an experience of stillness and thought-free relaxation into daily life.

Two autobiographical works by the author are available:

Autobiography of a Spiritually Incorrect Mystic, St Martins Press, New York (book and eBook)

Glimpses of a Golden Childhood, OSHO Media International, Pune, India (book and eBook)

Osho International Meditation Resort

Each year the Meditation Resort welcomes thousands of people from more than 100 countries. The unique campus provides an opportunity for a direct personal experience of a new way of living – with more awareness, relaxation, celebration and creativity. A great variety of around-the-clock and around-the-year program options are available. Doing nothing and just relaxing is one of them!

All of the programs are based on Osho's vision of 'Zorba the Buddha' – a qualitatively new kind of human being who is able *both* to participate creatively in everyday life *and* to relax into silence and meditation.

Location

Located 100 miles southeast of Mumbai in the thriving modern city of Pune, India, the OSHO International Meditation Resort is a holiday destination with a difference. The Meditation Resort is spread over 28 acres of spectacular gardens in a beautiful tree-lined residential area.

OSHO Meditations

A full daily schedule of meditations for every type of person includes both traditional and revolutionary methods, and particularly the OSHO Active Meditations™. The daily meditation program takes place in what must be the world's largest meditation hall, the OSHO Auditorium.

OSHO Multiversity

Individual sessions, courses and workshops cover everything from creative arts to holistic health, personal transformation, relationship and life transition, transforming meditation into a lifestyle for life and work, esoteric sciences, and the "Zen" approach to sports and recreation. The secret of the OSHO Multiversity's success lies in the fact that all its programs are combined with meditation, supporting the understanding that as human beings we are far more than the sum of our parts.

OSHO Basho Spa

The luxurious Basho Spa provides for leisurely open-air swimming surrounded by trees and tropical green. The uniquely styled, spacious Jacuzzi, the saunas, gym, tennis courts...all these are enhanced by their stunningly beautiful setting.

Cuisine

A variety of different eating areas serve delicious Western, Asian and Indian vegetarian food – most of it organically grown especially for the Meditation Resort. Breads and cakes are baked in the resort's own bakery.

Night life

There are many evening events to choose from – dancing being at the top of the list! Other activities include full-moon meditations beneath the stars, variety shows, music performances and meditations for daily life.

Facilities

You can buy all of your basic necessities and toiletries in the Galleria. The Multimedia Gallery sells a large range of OSHO media products. There is also a bank, a travel agency and a Cyber Café on-campus. For those who enjoy shopping, Pune provides all the options, ranging from traditional and ethnic Indian products to all of the global brand-name stores.

Accommodation

You can choose to stay in the elegant rooms of the OSHO Guesthouse, or for longer stays on campus you can select one of the OSHO Living-In programs. Additionally there is a plentiful variety of nearby hotels and serviced apartments.

www.osho.com/meditationresort
www.osho.com/guesthouse
www.osho.com/livingin

Books by Osho in English

Early Discourses and Writings
The Art of Living
Astrology
Breaking All Boundaries
Compassion and Revolution
A Cup of Tea
Dimensions beyond the Known
Earthen Lamps
The Eternal Quest
Flowers of Love
From Sex to Superconsciousness
The Great Challenge
Hidden Mysteries
I Am the Gate
The Independent Mind
Into the Void
Keys to a New Life
Life Is a Soap Bubble
Love Letters to Life
New Dimensions of Yoga
The Path of Meditation
The Psychology of the Esoteric
Religion's Expiration Date
The Search for Peace
Seeds of Wisdom
Silence: The Message of Your Being
Work Is Love Made Visible
Three Steps to Awakening
Into the Void

Meditation
And Now and Here
In Search of the Miraculous
Meditation: The Art of Ecstasy
Meditation: The First and Last Freedom
The Inner Journey
The Perfect Way

Buddha and Buddhist Masters
The Book of Wisdom
The Dhammapada: The Way of the Buddha(Vols 1-12)
The Diamond Sutra
The Discipline of Transcendence (Vols 1-4)
The Heart Sutra

Indian Mystics
Bliss:Living beyond Happiness and Misery (Shiv Sutras)
Die O Yogi Die (Gorakh)
Enlightenment: The Only Revolution (Ashtavakra)
Krishna: The Man and His Philosophy
Showering without Clouds (Sahajo)
The True Name (Vols 1&2) (Nanak)
The Last Morning Star (Daya)
The Song of Ecstasy (Adi Shankara)

Baul Mystics
The Beloved (Vols 1 & 2)
Kabir

The Divine Melody
Ecstasy: The Forgotten Language
The Fabric of Life
The Fish in the Sea Is Not Thirsty
The Great Secret
The Guest
The Path of Love
The Revolution

Jesus and Christian Mystics
Come Follow to You (Vols 1-4)
I Say Unto You (Vols 1 & 2)
The Mustard Seed
Theologia Mystica

Jewish Mystics
The Art of Dying
The True Sage

Western Mystics
Guida Spirituale (*Desiderata*)
The Great Challenge (Treatise of St. Dionysius)
The Hidden Harmony (Heraclitus)
The New Alchemy: To Turn You On (Mabel Collins' *Light on the Path*)
Philosophia Perennis (Vols 1 & 2) (*The Golden Verses of Pythagoras*)
Reflections on Kahlil Gibran's *The Prophet*
Theologica Mystica
Zarathustra: A God That Can Dance (Nietzsche's *Thus Spake Zarathustra*)
Zarathustra: The Laughing Prophet (Nietzsche's *Thus Spake Zarathustra*)
The Voice of Silence (Mabel Collins' *Light on the Path*)

Sufism
Just Like That
The Perfect Master (Vols 1 & 2)
The Secret
Sufis: The People of the Path (Vols 1 & 2)
Unio Mystica (Vols 1 & 2)
Until You Die
The Wisdom of the Sands (Vols 1 & 2)

Tantra
Tantra: The Supreme Understanding
The Tantra Experience: The Royal Song of Saraha (same as Tantra Vision, Vol. 1)
Tantric Transformation: The Royal Song of Saraha (same as Tantra Vision, Vol. 2)
The Book of Secrets: Vigyan Bhairav Tantra
The Upanishads
Behind a Thousand Names (Nirvana Upanishad)
Finger Pointing to the Moon (Adhyatma Upanishad)
Flight of the Alone to the Alone (Kaivalya Upanishad)
The Heartbeat of the Absolute (Ishavasya Upanishad)
I Am That (Isa Upanishad)
The Message beyond Words (Kathopanishad)
Philosophia Ultima (Mandukya Upanishad)
The Supreme Doctrine (Kenopanishad)
That Art Thou (Sarvasar Upanishad, Kaivalya Upanishad, Adhyatma Upanishad)
The Ultimate Alchemy (Vols 1 & 2) (Atma Pooja Upanishad)
Vedanta: Seven Steps to Samadhi (Akshaya Upanishad)
The Way beyond Any Way (Sarvasar Upanishad)

Tao
The Empty Boat

The Secret of Secrets
Tao: The Golden Gate (Vols 1 & 2)
Tao: The Pathless Path (Vols 1 & 2)
Tao: The Three Treasures (Vols 1-4)
When the Shoe Fits

Yoga
Yoga: The Science of the Soul (Vols 1-10)
-The Path of Yoga (Vol.1)
-The Heart of Yoga (Vol.2)
-Yoga: The Mystery beyond Mind (Vol.3)
-The Alchemy of Yoga (Vol.4)
-Yoga: A New Direction (Vol.5)
-Essence of Yoga (Vol.6)
-Yoga: The Science of Living (Vol.7)
-Secrets of Yoga (Vol.8)
-Yoga: The Path to Liberation (Vol.9)
-Yoga: The Supreme Science (Vol.10)

Zen and Zen Masters
Ah, This!
Ancient Music in the Pines
And the Flowers Showered…
And the Grass Grows By Itself…
A Bird on the Wing
Bodhidharma: The Greatest Zen Master
The Buddha: The Emptiness of the Heart
Christianity, the Deadliest Poison and Zen, the Antidote to All Poisons
Communism and Zen Fire, Zen Wind
Dang Dang Doko Dang
The First Principle
God Is Dead: Now Zen Is the Only Living Truth
The Great Zen Master Ta Hui
Hsin Hsin Ming: The Book of Nothing
I Celebrate Myself: God Is No Where, Life Is Now Here
Kyozan: A True Man of Zen
The Language of Existence
Live Zen
The Miracle
Nirvana: The Last Nightmare
No Mind: The Flowers of Eternity
No Water, No Moon
One Seed Makes the Whole Earth Green
The Original Man
Returning to the Source
The Search: Talks on the 10 Bulls of Zen
A Sudden Clash of Thunder
The Sun Rises in the Evening
Take it Easy
This. This. A Thousand Times This
This Very Body the Buddha
Turning In
Walking in Zen, Sitting in Zen
The White Lotus
Yakusan: Straight to the Point of Enlightenment
The Zen Manifesto: Freedom from Oneself
Zen: The Diamond Thunderbolt
Zen: The Mystery and the Poetry of the Beyond
Zen: The Path of Paradox (Vols 1-3)
Zen: The Quantum Leap from Mind to No-Mind
Zen: The Solitary Bird, Cuckoo of the Forest
Zen: The Special Transmission

Osho: On the Ancient Masters of Zen
Dogen: The Zen Master
Hyakujo: The Everest of Zen – With Basho's haikus
Isan: No Footprints in the Blue Sky
Joshu: The Lion's Roar
Ma Tzu: The Empty Mirror

Nansen: The Point of Departure
Rinzai: Master of the Irrational

Responses to Questions
Be Still and Know
Beyond Enlightenment (Talks in Bombay)
Beyond Psychology (Talks in Uruguay)
Come, Come, Yet Again Come
From Bondage to Freedom
From Darkness to Light
From Death to Deathlessness
From Ignorance to Innocence
From Misery to Enlightenment
From Personality to Individuality
From the False to the Truth
From Unconsciousness to Consciousness
The Goose Is Out
The Great Pilgrimage: From Here to Here
The Invitation
Light on the Path (Talks in the Himalayas)
My Way: The Way of the White Clouds
Nowhere to Go but In
The Osho Upanishad (Talks in Bombay)
The Path of the Mystic (Talks in Uruguay)
The Razor's Edge
Sermons in Stones (Talks in Bombay)
Socrates Poisoned Again After 25 Centuries (Talks in Greece)
The Sword and the Lotus (Talks in the Himalayas)
Transmission of the Lamp (Talks in Uruguay)
Walk without Feet, Fly without Wings and Think without Mind
The Wild Geese and the Water
Yaa-Hoo! The Mystic Rose
Zen: Zest, Zip, Zap and Zing

Osho's Vision for the World
The Golden Future
The Hidden Splendor
The New Dawn
The Rebel
The Rebellious Spirit

The Mantra Series
Hari Om Tat Sat
Om Mani Padme Hum
Om Shantih Shantih Shantih
Sat Chit Anand
Satyam Shivam Sundaram

Personal Glimpses
Books I Have Loved
Glimpses of a Golden Childhood
Notes of a Madman

Interviews with the World Press
The Man of Truth: A Majority of One

For any information about OSHO Books, please contact:

OSHO Media International
17 Koregaon Park, Pune – 411001, MS, India
Phone: +91-20-66019999 Fax: +91-20-66019990
E-mail: distribution@osho.net
Website: http://www.osho.com

For More Information

For a full selection of OSHO multilingual online destinations, see osho.com/allaboutosho

The official and comprehensive website of OSHO International is osho.com

For more OSHO unique content and formats see:

- OSHO Active Meditations: osho.com/meditate
- iOsho, a bouquet of digital OSHO experiences featuring OSHO Zen Tarot, TV, Library, Horoscope, eGreetings and Radio. Please take a moment to do a one time registration which will allow you a universal login. Registration is free and open to anyone with a valid email address: osho.com/iosho
- The OSHO online shop: osho.com/shop
- Visit the OSHO International Meditation Resort: osho.com/visit
- Contribute in the OSHO Translation Project:oshotalks.com
- Read the OSHO Newsletters: osho.com/NewsLetters
- Watch OSHO on YouTube: youtube.com/user/OSHOInternational
- Follow OSHO on Facebook: facebook.com/osho.international.meditation.resort
- and Twitter: twitter.com/OSHO

Thank you for buying this OSHO book.